'Living Your Dream Forever' through the University of Life

The Only Life Guide You Will Ever Need

'Living Your Dream Forever' through the University of Life

The Only Life Guide You Will Ever Need

David Jones and Jean Sinnett

BOOKS

Winchester, UK
Washington, USA

First published by O-Books, 2011
O-Books is an imprint of John Hunt Publishing Ltd., Laurel House, Station Approach,
Alresford, Hants, SO24 9JH, UK
office1@o-books.net
www.o-books.com

For distributor details and how to order please visit the 'Ordering' section on our website.

Text copyright: David Jones and Jean Sinnett 2010

ISBN: 978 1 84694 518 2

A CIP catalogue record for this book is available from the British Library.

Design: Lee Nash

Printed in the UK by CPI Antony Rowe
Printed in the USA by Offset Paperback Mfrs, Inc

We operate a distinctive and ethical publishing philosophy in all
areas of our business, from our global network of authors to
production and worldwide distribution.

CONTENTS

Jean and David wish to acknowledge their grateful thanks to everyone who helped in all stages of writing this book.

In particular we wish to thank:

Christine Cleobury for her wonderful poem 'Courage of the Heart.'

Mary Cross whose advice and guidance has been so helpful.

The staff at the Central Television Studios, Gas Street, Birmingham who looked after us so well and made us very welcome. We are indebted to their technical help and expertise with regard to the television studio scenes.

BBC Radio Shropshire.

Courage of the Heart

Good for you for going out and getting a dream with a
rainbow's end.
Good for you for trusting and believing that the universe could
be your friend.
Good for you for not stopping when things became real tough,
For knowing all things are possible despite the obstacles in
your path.
It's always the journey that's important, the fun and hardship
along the way,
The learning curve that teaches you the value in the day.
The leap of faith that creates it all and shows you what's inside,
That keeps you trusting in the heart and teaches you how to fly.

Christine Cleobury

For my good friends, Jean and David.
Wishing you both the best of luck.
Christine

The Campus

Imagine living the life of your dreams.

Impossible, do we hear you say? Don't have the academic qualifications to achieve anything? Want to learn new life skills but don't know where to start? See others being successful and wonder why it can't be you? Acquired armfuls of certificates and qualifications but still not where you want to be?

Then read on, because this book was written for you. Few people have the ability or opportunity to achieve high academic qualifications. Even with academic status there is no guarantee of lifetime success these days. Nevertheless everyone, without exception, can study, nurture, improve and achieve the highest personal development standards to achieve that 'life of your dreams.' That includes you.

We are talking about the core skills that make you the 'you that you are.' The 'you' that we see every day; the 'you' that portrays your own individual image; the 'you' that achieves that loving relationship; the 'you' that passes the interview for that dream job and the 'you' that climbs the ladder of success.

It is also 'you' that has to cope with the downs in life which strengthens your character, despite all the odds; the 'you' that has to accept failure and criticism; the 'you' that cries quietly when alone, but smiles to hide the pain.

Never forget that there is only one of you, unique and individual and deserving success. It is just a matter of realising that if you want to change some of your core skills or want to learn new ones, then you can certainly do something about it.

We did.

Neither of us, Jean Sinnett or David Jones, achieved many academic qualifications but have nevertheless fashioned successful careers in our chosen fields by concentrating on our individual life and people skills, learning them from the University of Life.

Jean is dyslexic yet always wanted to write a book, and she has. 'To compensate for my dyslexia I had to concentrate all my efforts on my personal development to achieve success. Originally I trained to be a hairdresser and eventually owned two salons before pressure of work and a growing family made me rethink my life. Now I am a Personal Development and Image Consultant, a qualified Life Coach and a Training Advisor.'

David was an officer in the Royal Air Force and, since his retirement, is now an Air Traffic Control Officer, a Public Relations Officer and a Training Manager. 'To me, life is like a live game of snakes and ladders with all the rungs removed! The secret is never to give up, listen to constructive criticism, learn by your mistakes, and benefit from constant improvement in your personal skills.'

Dreams can change over time, take different shapes; different directions. You only have to read about us to see that our lives have been continually changing and developing. So why not yours too?

And what of your success? That surely will be achieved when you are living your life in your own way, reaching the goals you set for yourself and being the person you want to be. With our help you can make that happen.

Welcome to the campus of the 'University of Life'.

Your registration is complete.

Your course is about to begin.

1

Having Faith in Yourself – Confidence

Confidence is the skill that enables you to hold your head up high on any occasion and makes you stand out from the crowd. Inner and outer confidence both give a massive boost to your personal self esteem which affects the way you feel and look. How you look on the outside almost always reflects your inner self. When you know you look good you will automatically feel and appear more confident. Remember, confidence is something we all desperately need and if you dress the part it is a great help. It is not indulgent to invest in yourself. It is essential.

Self esteem is an essential part of personal confidence. At the very root of your self esteem are your beliefs about who you really are. Some of these beliefs are accurate; for example nationality, age and colouring. Others could be just opinions about yourself, mainly based on past experiences. If those past experiences were mostly negative, then you have probably grown up with low self esteem. A good way to assess your self esteem is to write a list of all the positive things you feel about yourself and then of course another list of negative things. Which list is the longest?

You can also tell if a person's self esteem is high or low by the way they talk about themselves. People with low esteem can be self critical, apologetic on occasions and possibly very shy. Others will be aggressive and pushy, having difficulty asserting themselves without being loud and rude. People with low esteem will often avoid doing anything that may stretch their abilities or operating outside their comfort zone because they are afraid of failure. They may suffer from self consciousness and be over sensitive to criticism or disapproval.

Always remember the most formative years of a child's life are the first seven years so it is particularly important that adults do not over-criticise a child. This could eventually result in low esteem when the child grows up.

There are several ways to help overcome your low self esteem:

1. Be positive - think positive thoughts.
2. Repeat positive affirmations - keep telling yourself that you are and can be what you want to be.
3. Use visualisation - close your eyes and just imagine. It is a fantastic way to improve your whole image and behaviour.
4. Become your own best friend - take your own advice and encourage yourself to become more confident.
5. Take more interest in the way you look - always dress smartly. When you look good you feel good.
6. Associate with successful, confident people - think about who your friends are.

It is a fact that we become like the people with whom we spend most of our time.

Remember the law of attraction that success attracts success. If you mix with people you admire they will inspire you to improve your 'people and life skills' and create your own success.

When you suffer from low esteem it is difficult to trust your own judgment, especially when you are attempting to achieve your personal goals. You must define your aims and list a set of objectives by determining what you want to achieve, how you are going to achieve it and in what time scale. Allocate your priorities sensibly and reallocate as circumstances change. Above all be positive in mind and outlook.

As a perfect example, think about the planning required for a party with a few close friends. You must select a suitable date and then make your 'to do' list, which will include the numbers attending, menus, drinks and background music. You then have to prioritise your 'to do' list in a time and importance order and be prepared for any changes that you may have to make as the date approaches. The overall success of your party will almost certainly be due to your initial planning and flexibility. If your planning and timing is correct then you can enjoy a very successful, relaxed evening in the wonderful company of your choice. What a boost to your ego. Success is a great motivator and confidence booster.

Being negative just breeds depression and low energy levels. When we feel 'down' we only see weakness and are very self critical. We have a natural tendency to put ourselves down rather than build ourselves up. What you must remember however is that self esteem is entirely dependant on the way we see ourselves. Being assertive is also a great motivator. This does not mean being rude or bossy but firm and direct. Remember you are you. Be aware of your strengths and recognize all your achievements.

Put away your negative thoughts because you are every bit as good as you choose and want to be. Concentrate on your life and people skills and seek constant improvement at all levels. This will increase your confidence and boost your self esteem.

Personal confidence is the cornerstone of all people and life skills. In essence it enables you to achieve the very best from your skills.

In order to improve your personal confidence you should think of a time in your life when you were, quite literally, the best. It could be after passing an exam, winning a race, coming first in a competition or simply being paid a fantastic compliment. That feeling that surged through you and convinced you that you were unbeatable and the very best. Never ever forget it! That feeling was supreme confidence and it had a dramatic effect on both your inner and outer confidence.

Just imagine if you had the ability to repeat that feeling on a regular basis, especially when you are operating outside your normal comfort zone. Well, it is possible, but like all skills it takes practice and experience. A perfect example is that of an Air Traffic Control Officer coping in an extremely stressful emergency scenario. To practice Air Traffic procedures and increase the controller's confidence to deal with such situations, emergency procedures are practiced regularly. In the event that the 'for real' situation arises then the incident is handled like clockwork in a safe, calm and efficient manner. The overall result is that the incident is correctly resolved and the controller's personal confidence is increased even further.

Everyone is capable of operating outside their comfort zone. Of course you don't want to do it but just think of the rewards when you do and the result is overwhelmingly successful. You have then taken a gigantic step in the right direction.

What happens, I hear you ask, if it all goes wrong and mistakes are made? So what! We are all human and prone to such actions. Dust yourself down, learn from your mistakes and have another go. Eventually you will succeed the majority of the time, and guess what? Operating outside your comfort zone has now become almost the normal. Congratulations!

Think back to when you learnt to ride a bicycle, a skill which would have been well outside your comfort zone initially, when you attempted to master it. No doubt you had a few stumbles and fell off once or twice before finally achieving your objective. Once learnt however it is a skill which comes naturally, with total confidence, for the rest of your life.

The same principle applies to a range of disciplines and activities. Swimming is a particular discipline where many people who were initially very frightened of the water have eventually made excellent swimmers. So, why not consider pushing back your own boundaries and practice operating outside your comfort zone on a regular basis. It will do wonders for your confidence. Jean is the perfect example of someone who has done just that.

She recalls her school years as being very difficult because she suffers from dyslexia which was not diagnosed until later in life. She always dreamt that one day she would write a book but didn't dare tell anyone because they would just have laughed and derided her. She left school with few academic plaudits but to make up for her educational failings she concentrated all her efforts on her personal development and has continually pushed back her boundaries. She just wanted to prove that she had the ability to realize her dreams and prove her worth to everyone, including family and friends. Now, she is an authoress and a business lady. All her clients speak very highly of her abilities, which of course increases her confidence and assertiveness in the most positive manner.

To sum up:

- Remain positive – get rid of negative thoughts
- Image – how you look on the outside reflects your 'inner' self. Invest in yourself.
- Comfort Zone – take every opportunity to operate outside your comfort zone.
- Aim to be successful – success is a great motivator so strive to achieve it.
- Be assertive – firm and direct, not bossy.
- Have faith in yourself – be confident. Tell yourself that you can do it.
- Associate with successful, confident people – success attracts success.
- Personal development – seize every opportunity to improve your people and life skills.

2

Reach for the Stars – Personal Goals

Setting and achieving personal Goals are the skills that create and target your life's dreams, aspirations and ambitions.

The ability to set aims and objectives is probably the most widely used life skill in daily use. Virtually everything that we do in life requires some form of planning and basically we are identifying what we want to achieve and the steps we intend to take in order to achieve it. To be able to formally set your own aims and objectives can really help to speed up the achievement process and the aim of this chapter is to help you, the reader, so that you can achieve your own personal goals.

It doesn't matter if it is a personal, family or business objective, most simple everyday tasks can usually be achieved without too many complications, but the longer or larger projects benefit tremendously from a more formal process.

Whenever you undertake a long term job or project it is important to visualise the whole picture. The best way to do this is to clearly define the outcome. Once you know your final goal you must then consider the various steps you intend to take in order to achieve it. Does this sound familiar to you?

For example, if your goal is to do up an old motor car to make the vehicle safely roadworthy and proudly restore it to its glory days, you will need to take a careful look at the vehicle and make a complete list of all the jobs that need doing. You will then have to put the tasks into the correct running order on your 'to do' list by allocating simple priorities.

The spare parts and materials required will be the crucial elements in your planning process and you will obviously have to consider your budget and the time involved to complete the job. You will know the date you want your vehicle to be roadworthy so you can plan your completion date and work backwards from there. Ideally you will purchase your spare parts at the start of the project and store them in a safe place ready for use. When you make your plan of action and your 'to do' lists, you will have to consider the priorities. For example, you wouldn't consider re-spraying the paintwork until you have completed the mechanical repairs. Once you have adopted an initial plan you are then in a position to estimate your timings for each stage of the project and remember to allow a little extra time for those unexpected delays. If your budget does not permit you to buy all your spare parts in one go at the start of the project make certain that you order the individual parts to arrive with you well before the required stage in your plan

Now you have a plan which is structured, within budget and allows for unexpected delays. It has a start date, several stages when you can check your progress against the initial plan and of course a completion date.

You cannot be successful with any project, however, unless you constantly review your planning which can change as your immediate priorities change. The long term goals are always at the top of your 'to do' list but the achievement process must remain flexible because of timing changes and unexpected events. Unless you review your progress it is almost certain that you will drift off track and waste your valuable time. Concentrate on the immediate important jobs but remain flexible and be prepared to change your plan if circumstances require it. Provided that you keep focused and allocate your priorities in a sensible manner there is no reason why your project should not be a complete success.

This book project is a prime example. We set our initial aims and objectives and our 'to do' lists were written. After a while, however, our priorities changed. We sensibly extended our research phase which created new additional goals, including planning for seminars and presentations. We set up a training company aptly named 'Sinnett Jones Training' and at the time of going to press we are undertaking personal confidence, assertiveness and vocational guidance courses. Basically, we reviewed our book project progress on a regular basis and changed our planning as the circumstances required. This reviewing process will continue as the project progresses and who knows how big the final overall project will become.

With large staff and team effort projects however you have to look closely at your working practices. These working practices include delegation of tasks, management of time and tasking priorities.

The art of delegation is a vital skill and you can achieve so much more when you are able to allocate some of the jobs to other people in your team. Sub-divide the tasks and then organise your team effort. If you are unable to delegate because some or even all of your team cannot achieve their allotted tasks to the required standard, then it is time to consider further in-house training. It is exactly the same with family projects. Children just love getting involved and can be allocated individual and teamwork tasks. As well as being an excellent teaching and learning process, it can be great fun for the whole family.

The management of time is essential and you must always consider the time factor when planning to achieve your goals. Keep an accurate record of the jobs done against those to do and if it helps make a visual graph which will enable you to judge more easily and accurately. It doesn't have to be complicated, just a visual indication of your progress to date, what remains to be done and a confirmation that the project is on time as planned. It could be as simple as two separate columns, one showing the 'to do' list and the other the dates the jobs were finished or expected to be completed. By using a separate colour you can include the planned time at each separate phase of the project. The visual impact allows you to see the whole picture and will tell you if you are on track. You must also make sure at the outset of the project that the overall goals are achievable in the time you have allocated for the project. Obviously there is no point in starting a project which will take longer than your allocated time scale.

Tasking priorities are quite easy to manage. Simply ask yourself if each individual job on your 'to do' list is still actually helping you to achieve the outcome of the project or whether you are wasting valuable time on low priority administration. This is one of the reasons why a regular recap is so important, to keep you on track.

If this sounds really easy, that is because it is. By allocating small amounts of your time periodically to analyse the way you work, you can actually achieve so much more in the remaining time available.

We say that it is often possible to appear to achieve forty eight hours in any one day. What we really mean is that you must try to achieve the maximum potential from the twenty four hours available by the use of good time management. We have a simple system that can help those people who rush around all day and exhaust themselves in an effort to complete their daily objectives. Write down your daily itinerary in advance, then prioritise your individual tasks by writing a list of them in order of time and importance, trying to plan it so that you never have to repeat a journey. By simply re-organising your day you can often achieve three separate tasks, meetings or appointments in the same journey. Your aim is to create at least one hour each day of free time for yourself. One hour each day equals seven hours per week which is the equivalent of one whole working day. You have now created fifty two free days per year which is probably the longest holiday you have ever had. Keep an up to date advance diary and with practise you can easily achieve two free hours a day. We will let you do your own simple arithmetic! Time management is powerful stuff. Use it to your advantage.

A word of caution. Tasks tend to fall into two categories: large important tasks and smaller, easier, less significant tasks. These have been described, for want of better words, as frogs and tadpoles. We all tend to tackle the easier tadpole tasks and avoid the larger difficult frogs. The result is that when we have completed several tadpoles we convince ourselves that we have worked hard to achieve significant goals when in fact we are only skirting around the edges. These tadpoles do not necessarily grow into frogs. You will never achieve your final goals without tackling and successfully completing the frog tasks. Identify your simple and difficult tasks in the initial planning stages, and, if at all possible, try to break down your frog tasks into smaller simpler segments and individual components.

When your project plan includes one or more frog tasks, our advice is always to consider all your options and do not just aim to work around the difficult tasks. These difficult tasks will form part of your structured planning and will be essential to the overall success of your project. Try to reduce each frog task into simpler, bite size chunks, effectively making them the equivalent of the tadpole tasks and aim to complete each segment individually. It is important to complete your frog tasks in the correct planning sequence, allowing you to achieve your overall goals successfully and on time.

Some years ago when I was based in Central America, I was given the job of moving emergency airfield lighting from the mainland onto one of the offshore quays in the Caribbean, David recalls. This was to provide shelter for aircraft in an expected hurricane and was a very large frog because of the size and weight of the equipment as well as limited time we had to complete the transfer. Due to the obvious problems of moving such a bulky cargo I had to consult with the engineers and then decided to strip the equipment down into small easy to handle sections. These were then air transported rather then shipping them because we were running out of time.

Although fairly labour intensive, at both the departure and destination airfields, we achieved the task quickly and efficiently. By utilising helicopter transportation on normal training flights, we also saved considerable shipping costs.

The message is simple. Be brave and always consider all the options available to you. Be careful, however, when you tell people that you are going to tackle a frog today. They may look at you in a strange manner and not quite understand your intentions.

Individual personal planning is helped tremendously by writing lists. When you write things down they are more likely to get done. It's all about intention and just by writing it on paper you will start the ball rolling towards making it actually happen. It becomes more real than just a thought and you will feel good about yourself every time you cross something off the list, having completed it. At the same time you will feel guilty each time you see something on the list that you haven't done and this will encourage you to get more things ticked off. Basically, lists are essential if you want an organised life but one word of caution: when you have to make a list of your lists that is a sure indicator that you have misallocated your priorities.

Our advice is to keep a clear desk, don't handle a piece of paper more than three times, have a home for everything so that you don't have to waste time looking for things and do not go up and down the stairs empty handed. When opening the post immediately throw away anything you don't need, that is outdated or just junk mail. Sometimes all that is needed for our lives to run more smoothly is to change our habits in order to relieve everyday stresses.

One very simple, yet amazingly effective method is to develop the habit of only having to do a job just once. For example, when all your belongings have a half way house you will live in constant chaos as nothing is in the right place at the right time. However, if you always put things where they belong straight away then you will remain tidy and by creating a more organised environment it helps you to feel in control.

As a business lady, Jean is very conscious about the management of her time. Ask yourself why you are spending your precious time doing tasks that you dislike if you are not necessarily the one who has to do it, she argues. As an example; if you hate gardening but like doing housework, perhaps you could do a swap with someone or maybe work a couple of extra hours at a job you love doing in order to pay someone else to do the garden for you.

There could also be financial gains from this way of thinking. For example I may arrange to do one extra haircut in my hairdressing business which might earn me double the money required to pay a cleaner for one hour. The advantages are threefold. I gain more money, the client may recommend my business to a friend which will increase my client list, and by doing a job I am good at rather than one I do not like to do, it boosts my self esteem, she states.

One of the biggest lessons that you can learn in business is the relationship between time management and training. If you teach your staff to do the job as well as you can do it yourself, you can delegate with confidence which leaves you with a lot more free time to grow the business.

Using a story board is an excellent way to help you visualise and achieve your personal goals. It is simply a piece of board on which you can stick pictures and written statements. As a life coach Jean is expected to help motivate people to achieve their aims in life. She recalls a lady client who wanted to lose a large amount of weight so Jean advised her client to make herself a story board showing the way she wanted to look in twelve months time. The lady bought a large board in her favourite colour and together they stuck pictures on it of beautiful healthy food, the hairstyle she wanted when her face was slimmer and pictures of slim people wearing the type of clothes she wanted to wear. They also added cut-outs of people doing the type of activities she had always wanted to do but found too difficult due to her size. Affirmations such as 'I am beautiful, I am happy, I feel wonderful and I love the way I look' were placed in between the pictures; they were written in her own handwriting because this makes it more meaningful. The board was put in a place where it would be seen at least twice a day and where she would be able to read all the affirmations. Seven months later Jean was delighted to meet her client who was then three sizes smaller, had a new hairstyle and hair colour and was starting a new and better job. Her new found confidence was amazing, she had a lovely new man in her life and she was well on her way to achieving her own personal goals.

Another excellent example of how to allocate priorities in a sensible manner and achieve personal goals, is the story of a man who decided to build a large conservatory on his house. With his construction industry background it soon became obvious to him that a self-build project would literally save hundreds of pounds. He researched the project, costed out the materials and decided to use outside labour as much as possible because it was far cheaper than taking time off from his own business. He identified his objectives in order to achieve his final goal, wrote his 'to do' lists and allocated priorities and a running order with estimated timings. Finally he identified the frog tasks and made mental notes how to overcome any problem areas. He then explained the project to his wife and asked her to be his girl Friday, expecting her to be the home point of contact, especially during the early stages of the project.

The first problem occurred when his wife ordered some incorrect materials and gave a wrong date to an outside labour contractor. When the man arrived home that night he was quite angry but quickly realised that his wife did not have the in-depth background knowledge that he took for granted. The next day he took her to a similar project which was under construction and made absolutely certain that she understood what she was expected to do. From then on she was excellent and saved the project time and money because she was able to allocate and re-allocate priorities herself as required.

The second major problem happened when certain materials were late arriving due to industrial delivery problems. The man had to consult his 'to do' lists, re allocate priorities and adjust his running order to achieve the minimum delay within the overall project. Throughout this phase of the project his wife was a great help because now that she knew exactly what was expected of her she was able to solve any onsite problems.

Finally the conservatory was built. Overall, the project was a great success and all the objectives were achieved within the projected time limits.

To recap:

- Define your goals – what do you want to achieve?
- Define you aims and objectives – how do you intend to achieve your goals?
- Tadpoles and frogs – identify the simple and complicated tasks.
- Keep it simple – try to simplify the complicated tasks.
- Make 'to do' lists – the achievement process.
- Review your priorities – constantly review the running order.
- Time management – make the very best use of your time.
- Staff training – train your staff to the correct standard.
- Delegate your tasks – allocate tasks with confidence.

3

A Visual Representation of You – Image

Know that you look stunning! Personal image creates that all important first impression. A vital skill that, when perfected, enhances your personal development and makes you feel on top of the world.

Never feel nervous again when meeting new people and know that you will always look great whatever the occasion. The power of image and style is quite truly amazing.

Image and style have been Jean's lifeblood for many years. She teaches both men and women that style is an expression of yourself which helps you create your persona. If you don't project yourself the way that you want to be perceived, then you are selling yourself short. Style is a form of self-promotion, it will get you noticed and remembered for all the right reasons. If you dress to impress, you will be taken seriously because it shows that you value yourself and others.

Through her classes Jean has witnessed just how looking good can change people's lives. If you are looking and feeling good, it can have a psychological effect on the way you behave and your overall confidence. Then of course there are the financial advantages of knowing what to wear, therefore avoiding those costly mistakes. Remember your clothes are your packaging. If you understand what shades of colour suit you best, you will look more interesting, as well as looking healthier and younger. You will look more attractive because the right colours can also make you look slimmer and taller. You will be surprised by the way your mood can be lifted just by looking in the mirror and seeing yourself looking fabulous. So if you are really serious about enhancing your personal image and looking to maximise your potential, consider seeking advice from a qualified image and colour consultant, it will be money well spent.

There are other advantages to knowing what suits you and makes you feel comfortable. If you know exactly what you are looking for you spend far less time wandering around the shops, trying on clothes that look great on the hanger but awful when you try them on. The problem is that so many people assume that there is something wrong with them. They think they are either too fat, too thin, too tall, too short or whatever else goes through their mind. In reality the items they have chosen are just not the right shape or style for them. Another big advantage is that when you know which colours and styles suit you best, you will spend less money but look and feel much better.

A few practical tips for the ladies are:

1. Show off your best assets. For example, if you have a waist, wear beautiful belts.
2. Disguise the parts of your body that you are not keen on.
3. Always pay attention to detail.
4. Remember that underwear is the foundation that you will build the rest of your overall look on. Make sure that you wear the right type of underwear for the clothes that you are wearing and always make certain that the underwear fits perfectly.
5. Accessories can either make or break an outfit. Mix and match. You can make a cheap outfit look really upmarket with the clever use of one beautiful accessory.
6. Sometimes it is what you leave off an outfit that makes it look smart because 'less is more.'
7. Ladies, as we grow older we need to look as though we are wearing less make-up even though it may take more products and more time to apply.
8. Always choose good value for money. Remember that a garment really costs what you pay for it divided by the

number of times you wear it. Buy in the sales whenever possible.

9. Don't sacrifice comfort for style. If the cut is wrong or it doesn't fit properly it will not make you look and feel wonderful.

10. Clever use of accessories is the quickest way to make a simple outfit look more interesting as well as individualising your look and personality.

11. Prune your wardrobe regularly. Only keep the clothes that you really enjoy wearing.

If you add the understanding of which colours suit you best to an understanding of what shapes and styles work best for you, can you imagine how good you could look and feel? If you also understand the Rules of Dress imagine how much your personal confidence could increase every time you get dressed? As an image consultant Jean believes it is very important to always wear clothes that suit both your body shape and your personality, but you must also take into account your lifestyle and budget.

In the years I have been working in this profession I have noticed a huge shift in my clientele, Jean points out. Initially my clients were mostly women and business men aged thirty five to fifty five years old but now I am getting far more career women and men in their twenties and thirties. They are contacting me for urgent help, not just to rejuvenate their style and learn how to make the current trends work for them, but they also want to know how to wear their corporate sharp suits and still look like themselves. They want to stamp their own personality into the look. They also tell me that they spend so much time in their work clothes that they have lost confidence in choosing clothes for their leisure time.

My job is to give my clients a huge surge in confidence through their clothes. If you look wonderful it has an impact on everything about you. You find yourself walking taller and altogether holding yourself better. You feel far more confident about starting conversations with other people and this will always give you the edge both at work and socially.

Statistics prove that if you get your image right, employers recruit or promote more readily. Employers tell me that appearance is one of the top qualities they look for. Research also shows that interviewers often decide within ninety seconds whether they want to employ someone. Another statistic to be aware of is that women who wear make up can expect to earn 25 per cent more than those who don't.

Whether you are looking to improve your image for your professional life, or maybe you are looking for your perfect Mr or Miss 'Right', just remember that it is not necessarily about how much you spend on your clothes but what you spend it on. What you buy must flatter you and make you look your most attractive. Bridging the gap between what you see when you look in the mirror and what everyone else sees can be very different. The good news is that everybody is far more attractive than they actually think they are.

Personal hygiene is also a very important part of your appearance so always allow adequate time for the process even if it means setting the alarm clock thirty minutes earlier. Looking well groomed will have a dramatic effect on the way that other people perceive you, so it is essential that you get your day off to a good start. Remember that regardless of your economic circumstances you should always aim to look your best.

One of the things I teach as an image consultant is Sumptuary law. This is the unspoken rule of dress which enables you to dress in an appropriate manner and it is taught so that you don't break the rules and therefore offend people by the way you present yourself. This information is a direct result of the way we look and the image that we portray; for example, giving the impression that you didn't go to the right school or you don't come from the right background.

The interesting thing is that as a nation we are all interested in image and it is because of our background and history that we are all steeped in Sumptuary Law. It goes right back to the twelfth century, when a man was appointed as the Lord of the Sumptuary and he looked after the King's clothes. This law created a ranking system indicated by the clothes you wore and if you dressed above your position or rank you were deemed to have broken the law. You could be fined large sums of money for breaking the rules and those fines were massive sums of money by today's standards.

This obviously does not happen these days but if we fail to give the right impression by the way we dress, we may still 'be fined' by not being able to achieve our own personal goals. We may not catch the eye of the person across the room that we would really like to get to know or we may get turned down for that dream job despite being fully qualified. The interviewer may not have been impressed purely because of the way that we presented our self and his subsequent, very important, first impression. This is equally important for both men and women.

The clothes that you wear don't just reflect who you are and the life that you lead but they also reveal your mood. We also have to take into account that the clothes we wear for our leisure time are not necessarily suitable for the work place.

Accessories are just as important as the clothes that you wear. Your handbag or briefcase is one of the most important accessories so buy the best quality you can afford, preferably in lovely soft leather. It can last for years and turn out to be one of the best investments you ever make.

Ladies please note that belts can really tie an outfit together and give a wonderful accent to your look. Shoes should be in a neutral colour, the same shade or darker than your outfit. Court shoes with a small heal are best for business and should always be worn with tights or stockings. Keep the high fashion for your leisure time unless you are employed in a non conventional environment such as advertising or the fashion industry. With regard to jewellery, your watch is your best investment. Rings should be simple; keep the sparkles for the evening. In business wear stud or small earrings and again keep the drop or stone settings for later in the day. In order to look less vulnerable, a simple gold or silver chain necklace for women and a tie for men.

Gentlemen should always wear a long sleeved shirt and black lace up shoes when wearing a suit. Business suits should always be black, navy or grey. Made to measure shirts are a good investment because, as well as having the correct collar size, a shirt must fit perfectly on the body and sleeve. Make sure that socks are long enough so they don't show any bare leg when sitting down and make certain that hair and nails are always trimmed and clean.

Always remember that the way you dress gives that immediate impression of who you are and what you stand for. Research studies have shown that well dressed men and women are judged to be higher qualified, more intelligent and more likeable than those people who are inappropriately dressed. They are also treated with more respect and are given access to better social and business opportunities.

Just as in the twelfth century under Sumptuary Law you can still be penalised theses days by inappropriate dress standards. Don't forget that it only takes ninety seconds to form 90 per cent of any first impression. So this means that you have ninety seconds in which you have not spoken, acted or done anything else but somebody has made a major decision about you. First impressions have a nasty habit of lasting a lifetime as we rarely change our minds when we have made a decision about someone. Research again shows that the major component that goes into making that first impression is outward appearance.

Image is always at the top of David's life skills list because it combines attitude, speech, dress and a host of attributable qualities. He remembers a time when he was on his RAF Officer commissioning course. His Flight Commander would individually send Officer Cadets to various locations including shops and offices dressed in civilian clothes to see if they would be addressed as 'sir or madam' by people who had no personal background knowledge. The Flight Commander insisted that Officers had 'presence' and their personal leadership image should be automatically apparent. The cadets had to continue this exercise until they finally achieved the image, bearing and presence for the compliment. The same exercise was constantly repeated on the telephone to achieve the correct speech authority.

David's son has recently telephoned from Heathrow airport about to board a flight to America and told his father that he had been upgraded to first class travel at no extra cost. He assumed it was because he was smartly dressed for the flight. Basically the upgrade from the airport staff was a compliment to the dress, deportment and overall image of the customer. This is, again, another classic case of why 'first impressions' are so important. When David related the story to Jean she readily agreed and replied that some time ago she and her sister had also been upgraded to first class travel, for exactly the same reasons, when they were flying to America.

In summary:

- Personal presentation - how you present yourself to the world speaks volumes about how you feel about yourself.
- Image and Style - create your persona, dress to impress it will get you noticed.
- Financial advantages - know what to wear and what suits you. Avoid costly mistakes.
- Knowledge of colours - always wear colours and styles to suit both your skin tone and your personality.
- Confidence in dress - gain confidence through your dress and look stunning.

- Language of clothes - speak volumes about yourself by the way you dress.
- Professional dressing - when dressing for the workplace abide by the codes.
- First impressions - so vitally important

4

Get Your Message Across
– Communicating

Good communication skills enable us to convey important information. Never be tongue tied. Know what to say and how to say it.

As human beings we communicate in many different ways including speech, listening skills, networking, press and media, public speaking and advertising. Other vital methods include the written word, signs, body language and silence. Communication is such an important life skill because it compliments our individual personal development.

To master this skill is a great asset because it is a matter of being able to learn to communicate with different people at differing levels. Just think about very young babies. They are very clever at communicating and telling us what they want despite not being able to talk and we all know how frustrating a small child can be when they don't get their own way. They will always find a way to let us know that they are not happy.

The actual art of communicating with people in life situations can be very similar to being a host at a party, a meeting or a networking group. Think of the skills you need to host those groups of people. You will deal with a wide range of people who all have different personalities and are in various types of moods. To be a successful host you must have the ability to sum up a person's personality quickly and then become the person they wish to communicate with. They may be humorous, shy, nervous, aggressive, quiet or even tipsy. You have to assess the situation fairly quickly and act accordingly. Being able to read the vital signs is a real asset. For example, reading facial expression, making eye contact, interpreting image and body language, listening to the voice and the words they use as well as being able to judge a persons overall character.

The next time you are in a group of people, try to assess the people you are talking to by reading the body language and signs. Establish rapport to relax them and try to draw them into conversation about themselves. You will be amazed at how quickly you can improve your assessing skill and at the same time you can also practise your networking skills.

Networking is a method of communicating that can be used for a variety of reasons including job seeking, career improvement, marketing, buying or simply making contacts. As people we communicate naturally. We make contacts as friends, colleagues or business associates. Many of the employment opportunities these days are networked as often as they are advertised in the media.

Our advice is to build up a list of useful contacts as you go along. You will be amazed how useful that list can be, generating excellent advice and knowledge as your networking circle grows. Networking is of course a two way affair. Other people will want to know you for your knowledge or contacts. It is like a human internet and the more valuable your knowledge the more hits you will receive. From a career point of view this can provide excellent potential.

In business and the workplace, communicating is vital. The first point of contact with any company is make or break time. For those brief moments the receptionist or the person answering the telephone is the company's sole representative and as we all know first impressions are so important. How many times have you telephoned a company and been answered by someone who is offhand and brusque, perhaps telling you to ring back at a more convenient time or when the real expert is in. Do you bother to call back? I very much doubt it. Due to people like that, the whole business could be in jeopardy.

If you are self employed, in business or about to start a business no matter how large or small we recommend an experiment. We suggest that you award marks out of ten every time you visit a shop, telephone a company or generally make contact in a business environment. Concentrate on the friendliness, helpfulness, standards of dress if appropriate, voice, professional or trade knowledge and any other qualities you would expect from that company. You will be amazed to find out just how many poor communicators there are out there and your results will almost certainly point to the fact that the really successful companies are the ones that have got it just right. In our business the only people we would ever allow to meet our clients or answer initial telephone calls are people who are hand picked, trained and motivated by ourselves. This is how important we think the first point of contact or initial communication really is. Our staff would have to be well mannered but positive, have an excellent professional knowledge, be well spoken and above all be extremely helpful. If they do not know the answer initially they would be expected to take contact details, find the correct answers and ring the client or customer back. It is a simple formula but it works. We have a rule of thumb that we recommend you to remember. The everyday qualification that is common to everyone is that we are all customers of some type or other, and as such we demand certain standards of service. When we ourselves are called upon to give a service back, we must always remember those standards and then try to give the best possible service to our own customers. It pays handsome dividends. Basically, treat other people as you wish to be treated yourself.

Jean states that good communications skills help enormously in both business and social life. There are three key elements in communicating with other people; opinions, assumptions and then voice. Automatically, when we first see someone we immediately start to form an opinion by taking notice of their physical appearance, posture and clothing. Within a few seconds we have started to make assumptions about them. Of course these are all non verbal, but statistics tell us that we all judge each other in this manner. Research tells us that the actual figures for that overall first impression are 67 per cent on the way we look, 26 per cent the body language and only 7 per cent on what we actually say. So the next time you have an important initial business or social meeting, concentrate on the way that you present yourself. I recommend that you use our image guidelines in Chapter 3 A Visual Representation of You - Image.

The sound of our voice is very important too. You may have noticed that when you are in conversation with someone you like who has a strong dialect or accent you may find yourself subconsciously mimicking their way of speaking. This is because we all want to be liked and in our subconscious mind we are thinking "I'm a really nice person and I want you to like me. If I sound like you, you will like me more".

We can tell a lot about someone from their choice of words. We all fall into one of three types of person; visual, auditory or kinaesthetic feeling. Therefore if you listen to the kind of words someone uses when they are speaking to you they will give you an indication of the type they are. A visual person will use phrases like I see what you mean or it looks good to me. The language used by an auditory person might be that sounds great to me or I hear what you say. A kinaesthetic feeling person is more likely to use words or phrases like I tend to use my instincts or I have a good feeling about this.

My advice to maintain a good conversation is:

1. Be aware of your own body and facial language and tone of voice.
2. Have a sense of humour but be appropriate and careful not to offend someone with your jokes.
3. Never interrupt. It is very irritating.

4. Be enthusiastic. It makes the other person feel that you are interested in what they have to say.
5. Try to see the other person's point of view as much as possible.

I also believe that we receive signs in life which is another communications medium. Some signs can be through the spoken word or something we read or see. One of the most potent ways that signs appear is in conversation, if you take the time to listen to what's really being said. An example of this was when my marriage broke up and I felt that I had done all I could to make things ok, but to no avail. Whilst I was in this depressed state I felt a complete failure and that there was nothing I was really good at. I also I felt that I was not intellectual enough to start a new life for myself. Then one day I overheard someone saying that I was a great mother, a brilliant hairdresser, an excellent colour and image consultant and that I had been running a very successful business for over twenty years.

She also listed many more things that I was already doing. If I hadn't overheard that conversation and really listened to what she was saying, I would have missed the sign. It was saying 'stop feeling sorry for yourself', be thankful for what you have and get out there and build yourself a new life. After overhearing that conversation I went on to learn many more skills including life coaching, leadership skills and presentation skills. These, of course, led to my confidence improving with the result that my life just got better and better.

We all receive messages in varying forms from the world around us and although some of these messages can be co-incidental they can have a major impact on your life. Have you ever had the feeling that someone you know needs to talk to you? Their name keeps popping up in your head. This happened to me once when for no apparent reason I keep thinking about someone I didn't know very well and hadn't spoken to for some considerable time. Because I couldn't erase that thought from my mind I decided to give them a call. When I rang she told me that her father had died the day before and she just wanted someone to talk to outside the family. Following that call we became very good friends.

Another example that I remember vividly. I am always a very punctual person and never late for my business appointments, regardless of circumstances, because I always adjust my planning accordingly. Although I never use an alarm clock I always wake up in time and have everything meticulously ready for the morning. One morning however I overslept, the shower broke down, the dog was sick and the telephone never stopped ringing. As I rushed out of the house even the car refused to start. Eventually when I finally managed to start my journey I was twenty minutes late but then got held up in traffic caused by an accident twenty minutes earlier. If I had left the house on time I would almost certainly have been involved in a major traffic pile up. Fate, coincidence or a sign?

Three totally different examples of how my life has been affected in important ways by virtue of these various methods of communication. My advice is always be prepared to listen to, read and understand your signs because they really can have a major impact on your life.

Another excellent communicating skill is to be a really good listener. Listening properly is one of the greatest gifts you can offer someone As parents we spend a great deal of time and effort teaching our children how to speak. We teach them how to pronounce the syllables, speak clearly and be polite but the thing we don't teach them is how to listen. Listening is taken for granted and yet very few people are good at it. When we speak we just take it for granted that the other person will listen but the level at which they listen could range from not at all to being fully engaged. We all know how frustrating it feels if the person you are speaking to is not really listening. I believe that listening is a forgotten skill and that it is something that most of us need to improve on. Developing good listening skills can be a huge asset to you both in your personal life and in the business world.

Our state of mind or how we are feeling will affect the way we listen. If we are depressed we tend only to hear the negative parts of the conversation, whereas if we are in an optimistic and happy mood we will concentrate on the positives. This works both ways, therefore, remember that the person you are speaking to will be affected by their own mood and that will determine what they 'hear' when you are speaking to them. Thoughts fill the mind all the time. Thinking speed in fact is in the region of five hundred words per minute and of course these thoughts can cover all sorts of trivia such as what to have for lunch or whether to pop around and see a friend. In order to listen properly you need to abandon all other thoughts.

Everyone has listening skills, but the difference is the level to which they are developed. Some people seem to be naturally gifted with great listening skills but I do believe we can all improve. Being a good listener shows respect for what the other person has to say. Even if you are a little bored by what they are saying, you must remember that is it important to them.

Listening effectively is especially important in personal relationships. Sometimes it is helpful just to let a person talk and it is such a comfort for them to 'pour their heart out to you' and 'let it all out'. We need to be able to judge however, just how sympathetic to be and when to stop someone just feeling sorry for themselves. In the business environment it is important to listen to work colleagues, staff and management. Good listening skills are essential in the modern workplace, whether it is an interview with a member of staff, a complaint, a general business or a sales meeting.

Try to practise your listening skills as often as possible, especially in a one to one situation. For example, establish rapport initially with the other person by being friendly and relaxed and then listen intently to what they have to say without interruption. Only speak when you are encouraged to do so. When you do speak try to finish what you are saying with an indirect question which will allow the exchange to flow smoothly. Direct questions only encourage simple yes or no answers which will stifle the conversation. For example the answer to the question "did you have a good journey?" will almost certainly be a yes or no. By simply changing your question to "tell me about your journey," it invites a flowing response. Like any skill, practice will make perfect.

As well as being a good listener it is also important to be a good observer. This means being attentive and sensitive to the other persons facial and body language clues. While you keep the conversation flowing by asking interesting open ended indirect questions, you can observe the body language. You will be surprised at the amount of information you can learn about somebody simply by observing them. Have you ever heard of the phrase 'people watching?'

To have a good memory is also a vital communications skill. If you can remember relevant information and mention it the next time you meet, it makes the person feel special. It isn't easy but if you can train yourself to have a better memory it can be a great asset. Whenever you are introduced to someone make sure that you repeat their name. This helps to lodge their name into your memory and also subconsciously tells them that you are inter- ested in them. Writing down people's names in your diary on the day that you meet also helps your memory and always keep a notepad by the telephone to record important business conversa- tions. The act of simply writing information on paper is an excellent way to improve your memory. As a professional aviator David is used to 'logging' everything and as he says "you will be amazed how useful that can be, especially when dealing with disputed business information."

Being human, there is a tendency that we hear what we want

to hear. "In the aviation world we talk a different language and have to develop excellent communication and listening skills", states David. Aviation phraseology is fairly terse and to the point, enabling the Air Traffic Controller and pilot to pass as much information as possible in the limited transmission time available. Although the phrases are fairly standard, as the listening station you still have to listen very carefully to each transmission to hear the message correctly. There is no room for error. There are only a limited number of times you can use the phrase 'say again'. Just to make it even more difficult the military and civilian phraseology is slightly different. When I held both the military and Civil Aviation Authority Air Traffic Control licences at the same time, I constantly had to concentrate, remain focused and listen carefully, David concludes.

In general business conversation it is also important to understand what is being said to you. Do not allow yourself to be intimidated so if you have any doubts do not hesitate to ask and query what is being said. Again the notepad by the telephone is very useful because if there is any doubt you can always read back your understanding from your notes and seek confirmation. Never be afraid to ask questions if you are not absolutely sure.

Coaching Points:

- Listening Skills - always listen attentively and look interested.
- Positive Communication - sound confident and speak clearly.
- Establish Rapport - an essential communication skill that will relax people especially in the initial stages of any exchange.
- Question techniques - develop the conversation by never asking direct questions with yes or no answers.
- Voice - sound confident and relaxed but above all sound interested.

- Body and Facial language - look attentive because it helps to establish rapport and encourages people to 'come out of themselves'.
- Memory - develop a system to help yourself remember names and essential details of people.
- Communications in Business - good communication skills are vital.
- First Point of Contact - practice your telephone and greeting manner.
- Smile when you talk, even on the telephone and always remain positive and helpful.
- Networking - never miss a chance to network and make essential contacts.
- Silence - there are times when silence says everything!
- Signs - read the signs in your life.

5

Getting it Done – Self Motivation

Jean teaches her clients that what we need to remember at all times is that life is about self-empowerment and self reliance. She states that we have to carve out our own path to success. No matter where you come from or what you want to achieve, it's for you to decide how you want to use your power to get you where you want to be in your business and personal life.

Remember, motivation pushes you into action, action breeds confidence and when you are confident you start to feel in control. You will find that confidence is cumulative. Once you start to feel it you will get more and more of it. To really enjoy life you have to be passionate about it and you need to grab all the opportunities that come your way. Don't be afraid of failure, think of it as just another step towards success. When you hit an obstacle, see it as a test of how committed you are at achieving what you want. Ask yourself are you going to just give up, sit there and complain or will you take a deep breath, work through the obstacles and focus on your goals?

For example, think about the real successes in your life. Did you achieve them without any problems along the way or, like the vast majority of us, did you have to overcome several obstacles throughout the journey? When you finally do succeed doesn't it seems like a big victory?

Jean continues, I believe that self empowerment and self reliance means that you see in your minds eye exactly what you want and then work out a positive course of action to achieve it. I do believe however that your thoughts and your heartfelt feelings are reflected in your voice and behaviour. Therefore if I tell myself positive things that I want to hear it helps me to believe in myself and to have faith in the fact that what I want to happen will happen.

Don't be afraid or too proud to ask for help. Most successful business people will tell you that they have at least one mentor and we can all learn from other people. A life coach or mentor will help you recognise your full potential and they will encourage you to see the best way forward. I know it can be scary to take a leap out of your comfort zone and it does take a lot of effort but just remember that life is a series of adjustments. You can make many changes along the way but if you don't start moving forward you will never get anywhere.

Think about the people who you could ask advice from and make a list. It could be a life coach, business colleague, friend, acquaintance, family member or somebody you really admire. It is always excellent value to sit down and listen to advice and guidance even if you do not eventually act on it. Life will appear to be much clearer and you must have heard the phrase 'a problem shared'.

Good advice and guidance is all around you. We recommend you to talk openly about your ambitions and aspirations especially to your family. How many times do you hear successful people state that they achieved the pinnacle of their career due to close friends and family support. They will help you to motivate yourself and overcome any obstacles in your path, including the doubters. Don't be put off by those people who don't believe in your dream but do respond to constructive advice and criticism and don't get angry when things don't always go your way.

Let's face it life can be difficult at times when unforeseen circumstances creep up and nibble away at our dreams. But if all sorts of problems are thrown at us we do have a choice of how to deal with them. We can moan and groan, we can withdraw and become depressed or we can see them as an opportunity to grow and decide how to solve them. It does take focus and discipline, but with new found confidence we can survive most things.

The reason we often don't even try to work though our problems is because we are afraid of the pain of trying or the fear of failure. Fear is the main reason for procrastination because we tend to just bury our heads in the sand and hope it will go away. We need to acknowledge the fear and really feel it, then just get on with what needs to be done. You will be amazed at how powerful you feel when you have done it and I promise you the fear is far worse than the doing. It is working through the fear that makes us stronger.

Can you believe that my biggest fear is the written word or using a computer? This fear stems from my dyslexia when I was a child. I was told that I was stupid, slow, thick, hopeless and many other damaging remarks, and yet here I am writing a book with help from an earth angel and trying to become computer literate.

I really hope my experience will help all those that can relate to this. I know that confronting our fears and solving problems can be difficult, but please just do it. One of the best ways I find to work towards doing something I am afraid of is to use the art of visualisation. This is just using your imagination to see yourself in your mind doing the very thing you are afraid of.

Try an experiment and imagine what you would look like performing a task which you are afraid of. Think of yourself successfully achieving that task in a confident way, picture yourself being happy whilst doing it and imagine how wonderful you will feel when you have done it. I truly believe in the idea that everything you can imagine is real, therefore why shouldn't you have a full and meaningful life? If you can dream it then you can visualise it. It's then up to you to figure out a way to realise it because it's all about your self-empowerment and self-reliance.

Affirmations are wonderful because they are positive state-ments! For example you may feel insecure or perhaps suffer from low self esteem and feel that you are not intelligent, attractive or interesting as a person. This will then often be reflected in the way you speak or behave. By repeating positive affirmations and telling yourself that you are intelligent, attractive and interesting you will begin to believe it, boost you self esteem and be well on the way to becoming the person you want or choose to be. It all starts in the mind.

Some people call affirmations creative visualisation because they create a far more positive and self loving image. They are positive, personal and present-tense statements which aim to change your inner and outer beliefs in yourself. Visualisation itself creates a mental picture but it is important that you believe it is already happening. By making statements and visualising you are creating a very positive and powerful technique to create and initiate personal change in your life.

The best time to say your affirmations is while you are relaxing or meditating, last thing at night before you go to sleep or first thing in the morning when you wake up. Consider writing down your affirmations on post it notes and leave them around the house as reminders because they can be great motivators.

There are so many ways that affirmations and visualisations can help you to achieve your goals in life and help you create the sort of life you want. To have thoughts and visions that come even half way to the reality can be a wonderful experience. To be in that bubble of excitement when it happens can be one of the best feelings ever.

Try the following affirmation and repeat it to yourself regularly:

I choose new thoughts,
I am a motivated, conscientious person,
I am willing to change my feelings and thoughts,
I choose to look to myself for happiness,
I choose not to be fearful.

If you want to feel really confident, sophisticated and glamorous speak up and speak out for yourself! If you want your independence and to be in total control of your own life, you must work as hard as you can, or at least as hard as you choose to. You need to take control of your own finances because this will give you the choice of how you spend your money, giving a boost to your independence. You must also find total satisfaction in yourself before you ever start looking for it in other people. You need to be generous too, because no level of success will give you true happiness unless you give other people happiness too.

Now in order to lead this kind of life you have to be determined and motivated. Motivation pushes you into action and you have to take full responsibility for all your actions. You must have high aspirations and you need to be competitive not only with other people but also with yourself. You must really believe in yourself.

You will also discover that other people don't always believe in your dream, but that's not important. You have to turn your own dream into reality with your own persistence. You have to be the 'get up and go person' in your dream. Certainly, there will be challenges, but the more you face up to them, the more your confidence will grow. Remember, persistence pays off so keep the flow going.

Anger can be one of the big obstacles and we discuss aspects of anger management in partnerships in Chapter 9 titled 'Love, teamwork and rapport – Relationships'. You will find that very angry people usually have low self esteem, lack self control and are always quick to lay blame on to someone else. They are also very poor at taking criticism, often brag about themselves and sabotage close relationships. If you recognise any of these behaviours in yourself, you need to realise that it is a huge problem both to yourself and to others.

As an individual the only way to free yourself from anger is to change your behaviour. You need to acknowledge that your outbursts of anger do affect other people and anger can be caused by pure self indulgence. It isn't good enough to have these out-of-control outbursts and then just apologise, laugh it off or act as if it never happened. Remember great harm can be done to others though your anger.

It's important to remember that it is ok to feel anger, but it's very important to know how to handle it. If we grew up in a family that was full of fear and anger, we are more likely to carry it into our adult lives unless we choose otherwise. Choosing to change this behaviour will in turn make us and those around us happier. When we are angry it's not usually that we are angry with what's happening, but we're angry with ourselves because our life isn't how we want it to be at that moment. Think about it, when we are happy we very rarely feel the need for anger. We should identify what triggers our anger, and set about learning how to handle these triggers differently. When there is stress, ask yourself is this situation really important and then ask yourself can I control this situation? There are many things that people get upset about that are completely out of their control, and yet they waste precious energy getting stressed about it. The weather is a classic example. It's all about the way that the brain interprets the situation. If you see it as stressful then you are more likely to react with anger.

If you suffer from a problem with anger management, try asking yourself is there any value in your anger or is it all negative? Is there a way you can redirect that energy and channel it in some other way? By changing your behaviour and getting rid of your anger you attempt to make your life the way you want it.

Recently, one of my student clients told me that his work colleague has major problems with anger management and loses his rag at the drop of a hat. This makes the working environment unpleasant and stressful and he asked if I had any advice how he could handle the situation?

I told him to choose a good day when all is quiet and serene at his workplace and then speak to his colleague. My advice was to be polite but tell him that you are reliable and quite capable of working under pressure. Explain to him that you are all part of the same team with a common aim and that there is absolutely no need to vent anger and frustration. Assure him that you will do anything to help him but you don't like anger outbursts and in fact it detracts from the overall performance of the team. Tell him that in future when he feels like venting his anger to stop and talk to you and together you will resolve any problems. The secret is not to be threatening but treat it like a normal conversation. Most people will respond to that type of approach simply because there is no threat.

This is a classic example of solving a workplace anger management problem. By attempting to change the behaviour pattern of the work colleague it will hopefully create a much better working environment.

David's belief is that we are all responsible for our own destiny. Throughout this book we constantly re-iterate that not everyone has the ability or opportunity to achieve high academic qualifications. We can all however shape our destiny through our own self motivation and personal development David states. The whole ideology of this book is that it is quite possible to advance your status and position in life by constantly reviewing, training yourself and up dating your personal skills. The fact that you do not have academic qualifications should in fact spur you on and motivate you to achieve the highest personal skills to compensate. Of course this is entirely down to your own self motivation. Think on! Even in the worst economic climate there is always a job for a smartly dressed, well spoken, reliable, honest, popular individual and team worker. Add to this, self reliance, good work rate, effective allocation of priorities and common sense; the actual list is endless. Your job is to motivate yourself and work hard at it. Grab every opportunity. Enlist the help of your friends and family. Never stop asking yourself how can I improve? Mix with successful people and learn from them. Nobody minds being asked for advice because it is actually a big compliment. So you hate the classroom environment! Well, the good news is that most of these skills can only be learnt outside the classroom. I have a favourite saying; tomorrow is twenty four hours away so let's get on with it today.

Everyone has the potential to succeed in life and you have all taken the first step by reading this book. Whatever else you do, take away our message that your individual personal development skills can be your saviour. Nurture them and always strive for improvement.

Now try a skills test which will indicate where you need to make those all important improvements. Write down a list of all the qualities that you consider to be important 'people and life skills'. Then assess yourself and your own qualities by subdividing your list into your good qualities and your poor qualities. Next, select a few people who you trust to tell you individually how they see your qualities and make separate lists each time. Finally compare all the lists and you should have a fair assessment of your own abilities. You will now know the skills which you need to improve and although you may feel your pride has been hurt remember this is an extremely positive move which will pay dividends in the long run.

Finally, in the future when someone asks you for your advice regarding personal skills and self motivation hopefully you will remember our book. Accept their question as a compliment to your own obvious skills and you will know that you are on the right track. Good luck.

In summary:

- Self empowerment and self reliance – create your own path to success.
- Ask for help if you need it – do not hesitate to seek advice if required.

- The way you handle the 'downs' in life improves your strength of character.
- Fear of failure – acknowledge your fears and seek the solutions.
- Visualisation and affirmations – use your imagination to create confidence and success as well as making positive statements to yourself.
- Anger management – recognise the 'anger triggers' and redirect your energy.
- Change of behaviour – free yourself from anger by a change of behaviour.
- Potential – recognise your full potential, step outside your comfort zone and grab every opportunity.

6

Motivate Your Audience
– Presentation Skills

Skills that, when perfected, enable you to achieve the reputation of being a motivational speaker and presenter to individuals and groups, both formally and informally.

Sock it to them and enjoy it!

You are probably asking the question, what have presentation skills got to do with personal development? The answer is simple; they are very important because when you have the knowledge to prepare and present a presentation in a professional manner, you gain the experience and confidence to stand up and talk to people. It is invaluable when giving a talk, selling, networking or just saying thank you to a group of people.

Most people can expect to have to prepare and give a talk or presentation, which involves public speaking, at some time during their lives. It doesn't matter if you are giving an important Thank You or Best Man's speech, a fifteen minute talk or a full blown business presentation; the principle is usually the same.

The aim of this chapter is to provide you, the reader, with a basic template which you can use to plan and execute your own presentations. In addition we explain how easily you can utilise the press and media to your advantage when notifying and advertising your own events and projects.

The first thing to do when preparing a presentation is to get to know your audience, the numbers attending and the location. You must determine the type of people that will be present and the facilities that will be available at the venue. Only then can you plan your strategy. Obviously most people will be nervous at the thought of talking or presenting to an audience but the more you know about the environment the more confident you will be. The planning stage is vital.

All presentations have three main parts, the start, the middle and the end. Basically the rule of thumb is that you should tell them what you are going to tell them, then tell them and finally tell them what you told them.

Start with a general welcome and establish rapport. It is vital that you get the audience on your side from the beginning. Introduce yourself, check that the people at the back of the room can hear you clearly and announce the title of the presentation. You must then state the aim of the presentation and the objectives which enable you to achieve the aim. In reality you are setting your 'goals.

The presentation itself should be logical, in a sensible order and above all be easy to understand. In the planning stage make a list of all the major points you want to make. Write down the main headings while allocating priorities as if you are making several small presentations. Finally join them all up making certain that the presentations flows smoothly. If you feel confident you can add a 'tinge of humour' provided that it is appropriate. It can help to relax both the audience and the presenter. The important thing is to make sure that you achieve your aim and that the presentation tells the audience exactly what you want to tell them.

At the end of the presentation you must recap and restate your aims and objectives. This is also the time for you to ask the audience a few questions to establish that you have achieved your aims. If time permits then allow the audience to ask their own questions.

Finally allow the audience to pick up any handouts and socialise with some of those present. In reality the end of your presentation is an excellent time to network and to establish valuable contacts, especially if it is a business presentation.

For exactly the same reasons that we stated in Chapter 4, 'Get your message across- Communicating,' we consider giving a presentation like hosting a social gathering or a dinner party. The success of your party always depends on your initial preparation, planning and your 'hosting' abilities. When the final guest departs the overall success of the gathering is almost entirely down to you the host.

In exactly the same way you will be hosting your audience. When the audience arrives you should be ready and welcome them. The presentation should be planned and timed perfectly. When your guests, the audience, finally depart you should be able to congratulate yourself on a job well done. Remember there is no substitute for good planning and constant practice. When you finally give your presentation you should almost be able to recite it without the aid of scripted notes and know you timings perfectly. Practise in front of friends and get their reaction to your performance. Even if they don't understand the content, they can comment on your delivery and body language. When you are alone practise in front of a mirror and check your facial expression. It is important to relax as much as possible and keep your hands still; we don't want you looking like a windmill. When you have prepared and completed a really good presentation it will do wonders for your personal confidence because it can take you out of your comfort zone and it is an excellent personal growth experience.

Now, using the advice above, try to plan a presentation yourself. Think of a subject which you will enjoy talking about, possibly a business venture, a hobby or a sport. Remember the basic rules; it must have a beginning, a middle and an end. Finally when you have prepared it ask yourself if you achieved your aim and got your point across.

If you feel confident enough you could give your presentation a time limit. For example twenty minutes in total with five minutes for the start, ten minutes for the middle and five minutes for the end. Our advice is to take every opportunity to practise public speaking to promote your self-confidence. Like all skills, once proficient, it can also be an enjoyable experience. Give yourself challenges such as time limits because it makes it more fun and of course more professional.

The use of visual and audio aids is a personal decision! If you are going to use them make sure that they enhance the presentation and that they are good quality. There is nothing worse than poor quality film or sound track and unprofessional visual aids.

They do not have to be complicated. Handouts, flyers and simple photographs make excellent visual aids and do not distract from the presentation. You don't have to use a computer but if you are comfortable using IT, PowerPoint is excellent. When used properly PowerPoint can add a different dimension to your presentation. On several occasions during our presentations we have not actually used the live IT but issued printed copies of the PowerPoint presentation as an excellent professional handout. With the latest Microsoft software both PowerPoint and Publisher are so easy to use and the choice of backgrounds and colours is enormous.

One word of warning. If you do use IT you must always check that the version of software you are using is compatible with the equipment you are going to be using at the presentation venue. It is a massive embarrassment if it simply does not work. You must also ensure that you have a back up and a 'plan B' for your visual aids in the event of an IT failure. When we are planning an important professional presentation we photocopy several printed copies of the PowerPoint presentation which can be handed out to the audience in the event of an IT failure. We are then in a position to carry on with the presentation as if nothing has happened and we are all singing from the same hymn-sheet. The first time we had to use our back-up system the audience at that particular presentation were absolutely amazed at the smooth transition from live IT to visual handout despite the technical problems. As stated many times before it is all down to the planning and preparation stage.

Returning to the presentation that you have prepared, now try to add some visual aids of your own. Basically you must remember that visual aids have to enhance your presentation not just bulk it out. You can use PowerPoint if you feel confident with IT; diagrams, photographs or charts also make excellent visual aids. Make certain that all your material is clear, concise and it helps to make the point you wish to make. Stand at the back of the room just to check the quality and clarity of your material. Ask yourself if you can you see it clearly, read it and does it enhance your presentation?

Just like Public Speaking, Public Relations (PR) skills are so important. I hear you asking could I possibly be a PR person? The answer is that you most certainly can. The ability to use your PR skills is a people asset and should never be underestimated in value. Conventional PR means meeting members of the public, giving presentations, speeches or talks and dealing with the media and the press. It is, however, a lot simpler than it sounds. We have already discussed the valuable impact you can make with presentations and talks. Local press are also excellent and can be a tremendous help to you. Remember they need you just as much as you need them. They have offices on your high street, are easily accessible and are people like you, just doing a job. Local news stories, business seminars or events, however large or small, are their life blood. Get to know your local representatives, tell them your story and you could almost write your own free advertising and publicity columns.

To achieve the maximum impact consider writing a Press Release. Despite its official sounding name a press release is simply only an information sheet normally presented in a straight-forward format. The guide is Who, What, Why, Where and When! If you are going to e-mail your messages then write it in 'lower' case for direct printing. Send your press release to local newspapers, magazines and radio stations. If possible try to contact them beforehand in person or on the telephone and always be available in case they wish to speak to you directly. This will achieve the maximum publicity and media coverage as well as making extremely valuable future contacts. Look in your local paper. There is always a weekly business or local function section so ring up the editor and tell him you have a great entry for his weekly columns. I can assure you he will be delighted to hear from you. Once you have achieved your initial press liaison expand your experience by contacting magazines, local radio and television.

TV media is very similar to the press and the same principle applies. Their local stations are always very keen to hear good stories of local interest. You can achieve very valuable coverage.

Like any other skill the overall success is in the planning stage. Make certain that when it is quoted that 'a spokesman stated' the actual statement is correct, accurate and printed just as you want it. Remember you should be constantly marketing yourself.

It is also possible to issue a 'Press Release' to advertise a project. It could be a local drama night, a youth club or a full blown charity function. The size and type of your project will determine your media targets. Press releases or information flyers can be aimed at a range of publicity outlets, ranging from simple village news briefs to television studios and include local press, local radio stations and business magazines. Again, get to know your local contacts in advance and always remember they need you as much as you need them. They always want to hear your story or future projects. Write your news release then send it to everyone. If you only achieve a 10 per cent success rate, although you should always target a lot more, then it is extremely worthwhile. You know the rules 'if at first you don't succeed then send it again' even if you do have to change the information format. After all it is only a click of the mouse.

Stick to the rules, it makes sense. In your release or briefing tell your target audience who you are, what you are doing, why you are doing it, where it is happening and of course when it is happening! When you have sent it always remain available in case they want to talk to you. That way you can achieve the maximum publicity and by 'responding' to their questions rather than just answering them you can pass the maximum amount of information to the media. With practise you will become quite proficient and really start to enjoy your new found role as PR person. If in doubt watch the politicians, they are the experts.

So how do you actually respond rather than just answer media questions I hear you ask? When you have issued your press release or information leaflets, hopefully you will be waiting for the media contacts to get in touch. They will know the basic information from your press release so when they ask you questions you must be ready to respond and expand the information. Do not just say yes there is a workshop on Thursday 20th at 7.00pm at the Mansion House, respond to questions by adding you, the questioner, will be aware that our Company (name it!) is a leader in this field and as you will see from our Web Site (name it!) we are expanding into the local area. You will be amazed just how proficient you become in the art of responding to questions. You will also be amazed at just how much information you can circulate with just five straightforward questions. In essence you are using the basic press release as a platform to gain valuable free advertising. This response skill is extremely valuable because you will be able to use it in many other situations including job interview techniques or of course if you were to become a politician. Politicians are experts at responding to media questions. They hardly ever answer the original question at all.

Like everything else the success of responding to questioning is all in the planning stage. Before you send out your press release list all the extra information you want to get across. Then consider the type and format of the likely questions you will receive from the media and practise your responses! Again watch the politicians.

This book is a prime example. When the project is complete we intend to follow our own advice. We will contact the local press, local radio and the local TV stations. We will also be in touch with libraries, clubs, schools and anywhere that groups of people congregate. You must never miss an opportunity to network and publicise your project. Always be on the lookout for new outlets.

Discretion is a wonderful skill. David remembers being inter-viewed by a well known journalist. He was asking quite difficult questions and David didn't want some of his opinions quoted. At one stage of the interview he started nodding. When asked why, he replied that you can't quote a spokesman nodding can you! The journalist thought it was hilarious.

Finally, return to your presentation again. Now that you have scripted it, added some visual aids and practised presenting it, consider issuing a practise press release to inform the local press that you will be giving a presentation or seminar on a date in the near future. Remember the basics and tell them who you are, what you are doing, why you are doing it, when and where. You can contact them personally, by e-mail, telephone or post. In the 'for real' situation you then wait for them to contact you back, respond to their questions and hopefully achieve a good deal of free publicity.

Our final piece of advice is remember to keep it simple (KIS). The main objective of any presentation is to get your message across. It may not be a big presentation with ample preparation time but a quick talk, a one-to-one sales brief or just an expla-nation of one of your projects to a group of friends. You won't always have access to computers or visual aid materials and you may not have any time to prepare.

We have tried to give you, the reader, valuable advice but

there is nothing, but nothing like hands on experience and trying it out for yourself. Take every opportunity to exercise your skills. Practise talking to people and don't be afraid to stand up and give a speech or presentation. After all it is only your pride at stake and practice makes perfect. Remember success is a great motivator.

Now here is a challenge for you if you are feeling really confident and wish to accept. Try a lift-brief. You have to imagine that you are in a lift and you have three floors in which to sell an item or a project of your choosing to a stranger. The lift button has been pressed and you are on your way. Good luck and KIS.

Coaching points:

- Host your audience – treat your audience like guests and keep them on your side.
- Practice – makes perfect! Constantly practise your speech, timing and the entire presentation. Do it time and time again until it is perfect.
- Visual aids – they must be good quality and enhance the presentation.
- Always have a plan B and backup - make certain the IT is compatible.
- Public Relations – you must network and make contacts. Use all your media resources including local radio, press and television.
- Press releases – use them to achieve maximum publicity and impact.
- Press release format – who, what, why, where and when.
- Question techniques – if you are asking, never use direct questions requiring yes or no answers! If you are answering always respond to questions and tell them what you want them to know.
- KIS – keep it simple.

7

Choosing the Right Career
– Vocational Guidance

'Happiness in the work environment' is a phrase that very few people are able to utter with total honesty. Correct and timely vocational guidance however, will help you to make the right choices and enable you to utter that wonderful but rarely heard statement,

"I love my job!

"I didn't quite hear that"

I said "I really enjoy my job!"

Whatever you choose to do in life it is very important that you make sensible career or working environment choices based on sound advice and timely research. Your working life spans many years so it makes sense to make every effort to get it right.

Any person starting out on a working life or career path deserves the best vocational guidance to be available at the correct time in the career planning phase. Even a good university degree or academic qualification no longer guarantees a job these days so the very best career advice is a vital ingredient. With more young people than ever now applying for university places and the subsequent debt levels accrued at the end of their courses, it is vital to ensure that their personal choice of career is correct and, just as importantly, is made at the right time in the educational curriculum.

Exactly the same principle of course applies to people who do not have the ability or opportunity to achieve academic status or older people when considering a 'life- changing' career change. It is so important for every one of us to choose the right employment environment. When you are working in the right environment, which compliments your natural aptitudes, then your chances of enjoying your job and progressing up the career ladder are much improved. It doesn't matter if you are a factory worker or a rocket scientist there is always the opportunity to better yourself or gain a promotion. By making the right choices for yourself at the right time, the chances are that you will be happier and it will improve your own status in life.

Let's face it, very few of us know what we want to do with our lives during those tender school years. Those who do know are the lucky ones and are able to chart their career path from an early age. The vast majority of people however, make hasty choices and hope that it will be 'alright on the night,' or continue in the education system hoping that the correct choice will become apparent some indeterminable time in the future. For all of them it is a very hit-and-miss system with a small percentage getting it right in the end. Although it is possible to change career choices later in life that opportunity is often limited due to the financial constraints of family responsibilities and personal circumstances. Some people spend a lifetime eagerly awaiting a release from the drudgery of their working environment and simply cannot wait for that elusive lottery win or retirement itself.

The solution to the problem is good solid professional career guidance delivered at the right time, early in the learning process, with a regular follow-up vocational guidance system. It is essential that this guidance is provided by people who have the right experience and motivation to give it. In many of our learning establishments however, this sort of advice is normally presented by someone who is filling the post as an extra task which is added to their employment terms of reference. Despite being well motivated, they do not necessarily have the core skills or experience in the wider world of work.

That advice and the format of it must be a combination of expert aptitude testing, solid career choices based on individual aptitudes, personality and ambition together with a series of on the job experiences. Contact should be made with different working environments which include companies, educational establishments and like-minded career professionals.

A tall order?

Not if we are to get it right and provide the very best career counselling for the next generation of working people. If that advice and guidance is not readily available individuals should make every effort to help themselves to make wise initial choices. We have made a list of prioritised actions that everyone should consider:

1. List your possible career and job choices – think of all the professions or working environments you think you would enjoy and prioritise the list in order of preference.

2. Seek advice from career professionals or people working in those environments.

3. Find out if any qualifications are required and the best way to achieve them.

4. Consider all the options available – leave school to get work or an apprenticeship, further education at college or change jobs.

5. Consider a sponsorship scheme.

6. Seek advice from educational institutions –schools, advanced learning centres.

7. Seek advice from the Job Centres – they deal with job search every day.

8. Get work experience through your seat of learning–this will allow you to network.

9. Use Sinnett Jones Training aptitude guidelines - attend a professional course.

10. Make every effort to seek advice and network constantly.

11. Seek advice interviews with employers – always worth a try and provides excellent interview practice if successful.

12. Talk to students who are ahead of you in the learning chain.
13. Be honest with yourself - can you see yourself working in this environment and do you have a passion for a particular career?
14. Research your chosen professions or work environment – library & internet.

There is a relevant saying by James. H. Barrie that "the secret of happiness is not doing what one likes but liking what one does."

Albert Einstein also said that "imagination is more important than knowledge. While knowledge defines all we currently know and understand, imagination points to all we might yet discover and create!"

It is so important that you follow your own path through life and not necessarily the one your parents, friends or even your partner envisages for you. Never underestimate the power of the mind. It is possible to achieve miracles if you put your mind to it. We emphasise that even if you feel that you do not have academic abilities and are considering a manual or labour intensive working environment it is still absolutely vital that you are able to make the correct choices. Many managerial people have started out that way. Just believe in yourself and constantly seek opportunities.

One of our recent students left school with no qualifications and worked as a labourer on a building site. He was determined however to learn a trade and better himself. The clerk of works gave him some excellent vocational advice and guidance and introduced him to a local building company working on the site. Because of his conscientiousness, general attitude and his positive determination he persuaded the building company to employ him as a trainee plumber. He is now the proud owner of his own successful company with several employees and loves every minute of it. His success is built on a good work ethic, sound professional standards and excellent customer service, which of course mirrors the ideology in this book. As he so rightly states, the opportunities are there for everybody, you just have to get up and grab them. Never stop believing in yourself and constantly seek good advice!

In addition to the self help list above, we recommend that you should make a list of your own personal vocational goals. Write down five to ten things you want to achieve in the next ten years and then think about the type of profession that will help you to achieve your objectives.

At the same time write down a list of all your positive attributes and remind yourself of them whenever you feel that you are not good enough or when the going gets tough. Remember that a gut feeling or hunch might be your creativity trying to tell you something. Our intuition is a sixth sense that we all possess so we need to tap into it and trust it as it will help us choose the right path to take. When you write your list of what you are good at remember to ask friends and family what they think your strengths are.

You must also think about whether you are a lark or an owl. Ask yourself are you at your best in the morning or at night? This can make a difference to the working hours that will suit you best. You have to consider your core beliefs and values as well because if the company you are working for has beliefs and values that are a million miles from yours you will never be really happy working for them.

To give yourself a guide towards making your best areas of career choice, try a simple self help aptitude test on yourself. This test looks at the way your natural aptitudes help you to select certain areas of possible employment. Firstly, write down your best subjects at school and then group them into either science subjects, technical subjects or arts subjects. Normally arts-minded type of people will choose creative or people and administration oriented jobs, science-minded people may choose a computer, research or scientific environment and technical people would normally choose an engineering background as well as possibly working with their hands. There is a natural overlap between arts and science minded people as well as technical and science minded people but very rarely between the arts and technical environment. Basically arts minded people will rarely have the aptitude for technical employment, and vice versa. Next, write down your hobbies and part-time interests which should confirm your findings. People who enjoy hands-on hobbies like working on cars and motor bikes will normally be employed in a technical environment. Computer buffs with similar hobbies will normally choose the science environment and people who enjoy art, drama and more creative hobbies will choose the artistic environment. It is only a simple guide but the results it produces are invariably correct. Although the test will possibly not indicate a specific career that you would be best suited to, or indeed not suited to, as the case may be it will indicate general areas for your consideration and point you in the right direction for the next step in the selection process.

Making the right career choice is so important for every-one of us because we owe it to ourselves to make every effort to seek the correct advice and guidance so that we can make those all important life changing decisions. Our advice is to seek out infor-mation from whatever source you consider relevant, talk to people in various types of employment, listen carefully to profes-sional advice and never give up trying to achieve that ultimate career goal. Your aim is to achieve that phrase 'I love my job'. You don't need to be a famous sports star or pop idol to achieve success in your life, just make the right choices and never give up on your personal goals.

Most importantly, if you are unsure about which path to take remember to listen to your intuition. It is that inner voice that tells you whether something feels right or not. Invariably the voice is right.

Coaching points:

- List your positive attributes – commit them to memory.
- Define your strengths – liaise with family and friends.
- Create your own destiny – remember the power of the mind.
- Listen to your intuition – your inner voice.

8

Take up the Challenge Again
– Women Back to Work

It is time to take up the challenge again. Or is it? Your terms of reference, your job specification and CV as a housewife and mother state quite clearly that you are a manager, an accountant, a disciplinarian, a team worker, a shoulder to cry on, a taxi driver, an organiser, a trainer, a life coach and quite simply someone to blame for everything that goes wrong; that is, of course, just at home with the family. Welcome back to the other world and please bring your qualifications with you!

Although this chapter is primarily written for women returning to work, most of the coaching tips will apply equally to male and female applicants returning to or searching for employment.

When you are considering a return to work you need to think about all the possibilities that are available and you need to be certain about what you want from the job. Draw up a list of all the factors that are important to you and also list all the areas where you could be flexible. You must remember that negotiating isn't all about salary. You may be prepared to exchange a lower wage for some updated technical training, especially if you haven't worked for a while. Do your research before your interview and learn as much information as possible about the company you are applying to. You may consider taking a position at a slightly lower level than the job you had before leaving the workplace to have a family. This may help you to build your confidence by gaining business experience after your break. The key to success or failure is your attitude and you need to be passionate about what you want. Don't be afraid to be honest about any concerns you might have or of the challenges ahead. To succeed in today's fast changing business world you may have to do things differently. Be prepared to think 'outside the box' and always be ready to take good advice.

It is noticeable in the business world that difficult times often result in changes in the way that business is done. Good client service is thankfully becoming more important and the way that staff dress for work is changing. Worried workers are at last realising that the way they look is important. They are beginning to replace casual clothes with a more professional look, favouring much smarter clothes, including suits and jackets. This projects a much more efficient image as it gives the impression that your clients and colleagues are important to you and that you are responsible, trustworthy and good at your job.

You may consider the possibility of starting your own business. This country is full of women who have the passion and resilience to get their own business off the ground. Working for yourself or for somebody else however, it is important to get the balance between home and work life right for you. Getting your own business started is not going to be easy but it can be very rewarding. There is no doubt that if you get the formula right it may be the best decision you ever make. The possibilities are endless, from computer-based administration, landscape designing, basic garden services to pet sitting and media consultancy.

You can operate from your home base, be flexible with regard to working hours and arrangements as well as having a totally satisfying career. Think of the wealth of expertise that you have and match it to a local or national demand. In this age of computerisation and communication skills, office location is of little consequence.

Try a little exercise for yourself. Write a list of all the types of self employed business ventures that may be of interest to you. Then select an area of approximately a twenty miles radius and write down the business possibilities that you could foresee being successful in that specific area. Finally consider the wider, national picture and make another possible potential list. When you compare your lists see if there is an obvious niche for your serious consideration and one that could possibly be expanded nationally at a later date. If so then it may be time to start an in-depth research. If you decide that your ideas have potential then you could decide to take part-time employment for a while to finance the launch of your business and possibly gain some valuable expertise at someone else's expense. When you are ready to launch your business, you have to write a business plan, however simple, and consider your lines of communication with prospective customers. Again, if you are really serious, take professional advice whenever and wherever you can get it. This is also the time to join a networking group to advertise your intentions and drum up trade. Many small business ventures are launched from home and do not require large sums of money to get started. Exciting times!

If you do decide to go down this route and you set yourself up in business, one of your major considerations is client-needs and there are several questions that you have to ask yourself. You must get to know why your clients would choose you rather than your competitor. Is it because you would give a better service, or because you would be cheaper? It may just be that you are local or easier to get to.

Different things are important to different people, but it is really important that we understand our clients' needs. We need to find out what they want. You're probably thinking that you couldn't possibly ask your customers questions such as 'what would entice you to come back more often'? or 'what is it you like or dislike about my products or services'? Also you need to determine what you could do differently to please them even more. Do not be afraid to ask your clientele searching questions because most people like to be asked their opinions; it makes them feel valued as customers. Basically it is good old fashioned customer service which can create that wonderful 'walking advertisement.'

In this day and age with restricted credit facilities it is easy to fall into the trap of believing that everyone is driven by low prices but it isn't always the case. There are many people who prefer to have good service and good advice. This may mean you have to spend more money on staff training but in the long run you will probably still be in business in years to come when the cut price businesses have gone by the wayside. In spite of any economic downturn we must remember that life goes on as usual and there will always be people who need the type of product or service you supply. Therefore, you need to make sure that you and your business are in demand and the one that customers will continually call on.

Everyone wants more value for their money. In order to get more you have to give more so why not let it be a better service that you give to get more clients? This may also be a good time to think about learning new skills in order to offer more services because you may have to think more laterally in order to survive any economic changes. If you have the passion and use your entrepreneurial flair you will be able to fulfil your clients' needs and build your business. It's a matter of fact that during a period of slow or stagnant economic growth, the strong grow stronger by outperforming the weaker competition.

During your independent job search and that all-important interview you must never forget that you are marketing a product. That product is you. It doesn't matter if you are a mum returning to work, a person looking for a career change or simply an individual looking for a job, the principle is exactly the same. Always market your strengths and turn failure into success. We are all human and get rejected at times. Learn from it and ask yourself why you failed on that occasion. If possible correct any mistakes but never ever give up. Remember you only need one job at any one time! You only have to achieve success once. Even during difficult times like a recession remember that although there are many people unemployed the vast majority of people are still in work and job vacancies do exist. By applying the correct marketing strategy for you the person, you will eventually succeed.

We have stated on numerous occasions that first impressions are so important. Your image, style and presentation are so vital. When writing your CV consider using pastel shades of paper rather than plain white so that it stands out in the 'pile' of applications and always use the best quality paper. Also always be positive and know exactly why you are applying for that particular job. Research the company thoroughly and know where you want to go in career terms with that company. In a controlled voice give snappy answers to questions but have your own questions readily prepared. Remember the interview is a two-way affair so establish initial rapport, give a firm handshake, be totally positive, passionate and motivated. Interviews are usually competitive so know why you are the best and what you can do for the company. Smile, relax but sit upright and try to enjoy the experience. Believe it or not interviews can be good fun and a meeting of minds. Above all else be enthusiastic. It makes so much difference because enthusiastic people are normally successful people. One simple exercise that we recommend you to do is to practise your interview techniques with a friend. Write down all the possible likely questions you can think of and set up a question and answer practise session. You will find it helps tremendously just giving the answers to somebody else and you will become far more confident with your answers.

David remembers when he was an interviewer. We would average twenty interviews a day he recalls. From the interviewer's point of view it can be quite a mundane job. Then, out of the blue, a different kind of candidate would walk in the room. That candidate would be immaculately dressed and walk into the room in a determined manner, and with a smile. They would establish rapport, know exactly why they were there and where they wanted to go in company career terms. They were extremely pleasant, polite, had excellent manners and could converse in a sensible way. At the end of the interview they would stand up, shake hands, thank the interview panel for their valuable time and leave the room in the same determined manner. Overall it was a very pleasant experience and invariably that candidate got the job.

That is your target. Try to emulate that candidate and never ever forget that this is a self-marketing exercise. You are the prize. Make the company want it. Treat getting a job like a job itself. During your job search define your aims and make a list of your plans and objectives to achieve your goals. As you job search know what you want by clarifying your ambitions and deciding what you want from your life and work. You need to know you, the product, inside and out. Know your strengths and weaknesses and list every possible question that could be thrown at you. Seek out the companies that could provide the career that you want and then prioritise the list. When you have found suitable possible future employers research them! Find out if they are recruiting or expanding in the future. Finally close in for the kill! Sell your product to them. You must show them that you will fit in, can solve problems for them and above all can improve their position in the market place. At the very minimum you must be cost-effective.

So how do you get to contact the companies of your choice, I hear you ask? Most job vacancies are networked or recruited internally because it is less costly. The number of employment opportunities advertised is actually quite minimal. Remember that your job is to advertise yourself and you must try all sorts of ways to achieve your goal, leaving no stone unturned. I am a great believer in the speculative letter. Write to company Human Resources (HR) departments and request an advice session. State that you are considering a career in their type of employment environment and that you would be very grateful for a little of their 'most valuable time' to give you some important advice with regard to your ambitions. If you succeed in your request then you may well have a one-to-one with the very person whom you targeted in your original job search. When in the meeting make sure that you take every advantage and market yourself. Before the end of the meeting. make certain that you ask advice about your CV which you just happen to have with you and as you leave state that if a suitable vacancy comes up in the future you can be immediately contactable. Make sure that your CV reflects the employment environment that you are discussing.

Mothers returning to work should be careful that they do not make themselves over qualified for the job. To apply for a fairly mundane local job and restrictive hours due to family commitments with a rocket scientist CV is perhaps not a good idea. In your application you should state that despite your high academic level qualification and restrictive working hours you really want the job for the right reasons and have the ability to achieve far more in the time allocated than any average candidate. You are then using your limited access to employment and your qualifications as a massive strength not a weakness. Remember always market your strengths and consider all the alternatives to turn your weaknesses into strengths.

Companies often need cover for lunch times, maternity leave and holidays. Part time workers are a financial advantage to a company because they can be flexible, often available at short notice and are not normally entitled to pension funds. If you drive make sure they understand that you are not reliant on public transport and that you own a reliable car. Point out that you have great family back-up and no problem with child care. Never say that you are just a housewife. Explain that you have great time-management skills and that you can juggle several jobs at once. You are expected to get the family where they need to be on time as well as being a taxi driver, cook, gardener and cleaner etc. In other words pre-empt all the negative questions that the employer will possibly ask with positive reasons for employing you.

In summary. Always remember that you are marketing yourself so ask yourself that most important question. Would you buy you, the product? If not. why not?

One lady student recently pointed out that her husband has to be mobile in his job so they move home regularly and whenever she is job hunting it is normally in a rural area where there are very few vacancies, especially as a working mother. Quite obviously it can be a nightmare trying to find work in those circumstances and you have to be totally resilient to accept all the rejections. Another student however, found her ideal job just a few steps from her front door in the local village. If she hadn't attended our course she would never have considered looking so close to home, so always consider all your options and try every possible avenue. Success is always where you find it!

Always remember however that your aim must always be to market 'you the package' in the very best way you can. In rural areas vacancies are usually minimal so you must make doubly certain that you are very best person available. Look at your qualifications and brush up on your skills. Ask yourself if you can improve by applying for courses. Attending courses to improve your qualifications indicates personal motivation and improves your all round appeal. Update your CV and make sure it markets you properly and that it advertises you as the right type of person! Your CV is your advertisement so review every word until it is perfect and reflects the person that you yourself would want to employ. Even 'on line' applications will require a life and career résumé which will be similar to your CV so it is important to get it right in the planning stages! Dependent on the type of job application you may need to amend your CV to match the job specifications or write an appropriate covering letter with each separate job application. Make sure that you check every application thoroughly.

Read the local press, scan the job vacancy pages and make sure that you read between the lines. For example, if a local company is recruiting several HGV drivers then assume that they must be expanding and will need more administration staff and other employees. Here is your opportunity to write or contact the company and state that you notice they are recruiting and possibly expanding so send a copy of your CV. Again, write speculative letters to seek advice interviews as well and always take your CV with you because you must market yourself at every opportunity. Constantly network in the local area and get yourself known. Networking will also tell you what services are available in the local area and more importantly what services are not! Ask yourself if there is a niche available that will give you the opportunity to provide a service to your local community and start that self employed business. Some of the local rural sleepy hollow organisations like gardening clubs are often run by local company executives so keep your ear to the ground. If you see an advert for your dream job, consider taking your application, CV and, if appropriate, a covering letter straight to the company and inform them that you are available immediately. Point out that this could save them the recruitment hassle. It may be a bit cheeky but it will most certainly indicate excellent motivation and personal ambition as well as getting you noticed.

It's not rocket science but a matter of common sense. Despite all the advice that we give, you must always remember not to leave any stone unturned. Basically try anything that you think may work during your job search and final success. Never forget you only need one job at a time so you only have to be successful once. Remember it is all part of a learning curve so learn from any rejections and improve. Look upon rejection as just a part of normal job search and always turn you weaknesses into strengths. Seek advice from wherever you can get it, network yourself constantly and always remember that you are advertising yourself. If your available working hours are restricted because of family commitments tell employers that with your skills they will be making a wise choice because you can achieve in a few hours what other applicants could not do in a week

In summary:

- Return to work – consider all the possibilities. What do you want from the job?
- Self employment – an option you could consider. Research the market and look at all the possibilities.
- Home and work- you must get the balance right. Consider your priorities.
- Marketing you the person – look upon yourself as an advertising package.
- CV – your CV is a vital and flexible document. Make sure that your CV matches the job description and consider the need for a covering letter.
- Speculative letters – 'leave no stone unturned'. Seek out and write to companies that may help your job search.
- Interview technique – plan your tactics. Thoroughly research the company, know why you are there and why you are the best person for the job.
- Always be enthusiastic – enthusiasm is infectious!
- Image - remember that all important first impression.
- Dress as a professional and invest in yourself.
- Training – grab every opportunity to widen your knowledge

9

Love, Teamwork and Rapport
– Relationships

Personal and workplace relationship skills are vital because they represent the 'life blood' of all human activity! Successful relationships can be rewarded with those wonderful human emotions, love, happiness, contentment and personal achievement.

Relationships can be complicated because human beings are complicated, therefore our ideas don't always coincide with our loved ones' ideas. Even when we disagree however, we can still be loving. We must remember that no one person can be all things to us, therefore we are responsible for our own happiness and we should always treat others in a way that we would want to be treated ourselves. Also, to enable close personal relationships to work, you need a creative spark, a shared sense of humour, respect, patience, courtesy and good manners.

Prioritising in marriage is vital, especially if you have children. Happy parents make happy children. Don't bottle things up and learn to compromise because this will help to keep the relationship fresh and happy. You don't have to agree on everything but a spirited debate is far better than pent up anger or a flaming row. We can always agree to disagree.

Jean believes that one of the most important relationships of all is the relationship with children. Often as young parents we are all so busy trying to make ends meet, get on with our jobs and perhaps still keep some kind of social life going that it is difficult to find extra quality time to spend with our children, she recalls. We can also get a little bored with the chatter of a small child but we must remember that they are little for such a short time. I saw a saying on a plaque when my children were small and I thought that it was really meaningful. It said 'if you want to spend something on your children, spend some time'. I was so busy building my business but after seeing that quote I always tried to make more time for my two wonderful children. Giving your time is far more precious than all the gifts money can buy. So ask yourself, if you have children, how do you prioritise your time? Could you allocate your priorities differently? Precious gifts indeed!

I also think that we could improve all our relationships if we were more aware of the differences between men and women. So many couples get frustrated with each other because although they love their partners, tension builds up when they think they are not being understood. We need to be aware that men and women differ in so many ways. They don't just communicate differently but they perceive, react, think and feel differently. The more we understand the opposite sex, the easier it becomes to live in harmony. One of the biggest differences is that men offer solutions and invalidate feelings while women tend to offer unsolicited advice and direction. A woman expects a man to have feelings first, communicate and then act but this is not the way that most men behave. Men are more likely to think first and then communicate before reacting.

Co-incidentally, at a recent personal development class, one of the lady students asked why it was that every time she asks her husband to call and pick up something from the shops on his way home from work he nearly always forgets to do it. When she challenges him about it he either snaps back that he has too much on his mind and can't remember everything or hardly speaks to her at all. Of course some men find it difficult to multi-task and men generally tend to speak in a short, direct, solution-driven and to-the-point manner. They also speak less 'small talk' because they have a tendency to be more literal and need a particular reason to talk. Therefore she was mistakenly seeing this as a personal rebuff.

Men and women also cope with stress in completely different ways. Most men like to have time to think things through alone. They can become so focused that they appear to withdraw until they have thought of a solution. This can upset his partner if she doesn't understand the reasons why. When a woman is stressed she becomes overwhelmed and gets so emotionally involved that she needs to talk. If we don't understand and accept these differences it can obviously cause friction.

So the next time you feel under stress think about your own reactions and the effect they have on your partner. Ask yourself if it is possible to communicate in a better way and try seeing things from the other person's point of view. You may find that by communicating in a different way, solutions to your problems become abundantly clear because you are both working towards a common aim and are both on the same wavelength.

Not all bad or negative relationships need to have a bad outcome. I think all of us, at sometime in our lives, have chosen to be with unsuitable people. Very often I think that this is because there are times in our lives when we are made to feel that we are not good enough for anything better. The resulting under confidence is probably one of the most common negative feelings that people experience about themselves, leading to incompatible relationships which are possibly better ended. These experiences and their solutions however can give you the toughness and ambition to really move your life forward. Also remember that nobody can force us to feel anything at all because we are completely in control of our own feelings. Our feelings come from thoughts, and our thoughts can be changed. When we are young we believe everything people say about us and some people carry on believing these negative messages all their lives.

One of the worst things anyone can do to a child is to destroy their confidence with negative remarks like 'you're not nice', 'you're not pretty' or 'you're not clever' and the poor child can grow up believing it. But when we are adults, for our own wellbeing, we must get rid of these negative feelings and forgive the person who made these remarks. They probably didn't do it on purpose but just didn't know any better with the knowledge that they had at the time. So remember that negative feelings are only thoughts, and thoughts can be changed.

Ask yourself do you have negative thoughts and feelings? If so try to think back and trace the origin of such thoughts because this may help you to understand yourself better. Once you understand why you feel the way you do then it is much easier to change your thought-processes to become far more positive. Just remember that it is all 'in the mind' and you have the ability to change it.

Anger and aggression can also cause major problems in relationships. I think it is important to remember that although it is horrible and frightening at times to be around an angry person, we must try to understand why they are behaving that way. I believe that anger usually stems from fear and frustration, therefore if we can listen to someone's anger with compassion we will learn where their fears are coming from.

Very often when someone is being angry with you they are just using you to vent their feelings about something in their past. This does not mean we should necessarily accept their bad behaviour, but it does help us understand it. Angry people often blame others for their problems but until they can let go of the past and take full responsibility for their own lives and experiences, they will remain angry.

What should we do if we live with, or spend a lot of time around an angry person?

We must accept that they are the way they are and that their behaviour is not necessarily meant to upset and offend us. It is simply because that is the way they think and feel. Basically, we have two choices. We may be able to forgive their behaviour because we are forgiving them for being who they are or we can remove ourselves from the situation. If we decide to stay we must deal with it in a positive way that is good for us. The question is however, just how do we deal with it?

My belief is that we must change the word 'forgiveness' to 'acceptance' and we may then find it in our hearts to forgive. We have to do this because we cannot make other people behave the way we want them to. The only person we can change is ourselves and if other people are just being themselves, what is there to forgive? If we don't accept them as they are, it means that we believe they should behave differently according to our criteria. In other words, 'I am right and you are wrong' and this is not going to result in an 'I'm Ok you're OK' situation. Trying to make someone agree that you are right and that they are wrong is usually a waste of time. Sometimes it is better to give it up, let it go and accept that the other person is not the person you wanted them to be. They are, for their own reasons, the person they want to be or at least they are being who they feel it is right to be. It is only after you have gone through all these thought processes that you can then decide whether to stay or leave the situation and do what is right for you.

You may also consider 'de-cluttering' the relationships in your life. As we grow older our ideas change and we often find that our friends change too. You might find that you no longer want to spend time with people who have wildly different views to yours. It makes much more sense to have friends that you feel happy to be around because if you spend a lot of time around depressed or miserable people their low energy will drag you down. At first you may feel a little nostalgic about minimising the time you spend with long-standing friends, whose company you no longer enjoy, but it will be for the best in the long run.

We should also let go of people that are not good for our souls. Not everyone thinks in the same way or believes in the same things as you do but this does not mean they are wrong, just different. We must also remember that no one really knows what is in our heart, mind and soul. They are not mind readers so it's up to us to express our needs. We must also learn to detach and give other people space, as well as respecting other people's privacy. We should honour each other's values, principles and beliefs, even if they are not the same as ours. Love is patient, kind and caring. It is never jealous or boastful, nor is it arrogant or rude and love never insists on its own way. Love is also generous and undemanding. We should mix with people who inspire us and make us feel happy.

As David points out when asked about relationships, most people will obviously immediately think of their personal relationships with loved ones. This subject however also covers our relationships with friends, work colleagues and staff, networking contacts and neighbours.

I have been an exceptionally lucky and privileged person, recalls David. I grew up in the heart of the Shropshire countryside with wonderful parents and a very close relationship with my only brother. I look back on my school days at the local grammar school with great affection. Although I was not highly academically qualified when I left school, I consider that my schooling was most satisfactory because it taught me the basic core life skills that I was to develop further in later life. I was taught the value of personal discipline as well as the importance of respect and good manners. Above all I was also taught the true importance of developing good personal relationships in all aspects of life and particularly in a career environment.

Managing relationships in the work place is an obvious key factor in any career success. Your liaison with management, colleagues, general staff, customers and clientele is a vital skill. Minor squabbles, personal dislikes and personality clashes make for an interesting if not totally friendly working environment but you must rise above it. Regardless of your working environment the ability to be a good team worker is essential and even individual self employed people have to consider the advantages of team networking.

In my aviation world the ability to be a good team worker is mandatory, continues David. On the flight deck there is no room for sentiment. You have to respect your colleagues and work as a team to the letter. This is vital, especially in an emergency situation, and a perfect example of how personal relationships work in an extreme stress environment. Air Traffic Control is an identical environment where you must rely on your colleagues implicitly and liaise efficiently. There is no place for a loner in this professional working place.

Think about your own attitude to team working. The vast majority of us depend on other people in the working and social environment and being in a personal relationship, of course, also creates a real team effort. If you are really honest with yourself, how do you respond to team working? Ask yourself the crucial question, would you want to work with yourself? If not, why not? It is only by being extremely honest that you can improve your attitude. Again list your good and bad points then seek advice from people you respect who have to work with you. If you are really serious about improving your people and life skills this one is near the top of the list.

Your business networking success is totally dependent on your personal relationship skills. You must have the ability to communicate with all types of people and be an efficient liaison contact. The value of your networking success is also dependent on your ability to sum up and relax your personal contacts in order to exchange the maximum amount of valuable information. I love the word 'rapport' which sums up initial contact skills. Take every opportunity to network and, as you progress and your networking circle increases, you will notice how more relaxed you are at communicating with people. As we always say, practice makes perfect

Personal relationships with friends are probably easier because presumably you would not be friends if you did not get on together. The important thing to remember is that you get out of any relationship what you put into it and, generally speaking, what you give, you get back. I genuinely believe that you should treat other people in exactly the same manner that you wish to be treated yourself. You cannot be fairer than that.

Relationships with neighbours are important to ensure the ambience and smooth running of your home environment. If there are arguments and disagreements the skill is to handle the situation in a calm but positive manner. Try to stay friendly and always remember it is very difficult to have a major bust-up if one of the parties remains placid and speaks gently.

I am always amazed at poor customer service. I never hesitate to praise good customer service or to complain about poor service. I am however always very diplomatic and polite when making a complaint, pointing out that good customer service is vital, especially at the first point of contact. I try to encourage any good points and aim to make the discussion as friendly as possible. Realistically I see it as a good way to exercise my personal relationship skills in a possible difficult liaison situation. In any customer related environment accurate feedback is vital in order that a company is able to provide the very best customer service at all times. I consider good customer service and liaison to be a point of personal pride and in turn it creates an obvious walking advertisement from satisfied customers.

Try exercising your own personal relationship liaison skills. The next time you feel angry about poor service, ask to see the management and politely but clearly state your case. Using the advice guidelines above, make the point that they should be delighted with your feedback and you expect them to respond accordingly. Remain polite but positive and always seek a solution from the management. If they take offence politely inform them that they are in business to provide a service and your feedback is essential to them. Again this is another example of you increasing your own confidence in a sometimes tense situation. Never loose your temper because a calm person is very difficult to argue with. Also remember to make positive comments for good service because it is just as important and makes all your comments that much more credible.

Relationship skills must be flexible and adaptable as required, be it in family life, with friends and acquaintances, business or customer oriented scenarios and a whole host of other important environments that you are likely to experience in your life.

We talk about first impressions being so important and of course with close personal relationships that is almost always the initial attraction. But surely a person's thought processes, habits, interests, standards, humour and general demeanour are really just as important because these traits form the major part of a person's overall character and it is that which we have to live with as partners in life. Relationships often break down because we don't really get to know the real person until it is too late and we are committed. Of course people mature in different ways and at different time scales as they get older.

First of all you must have a relationship with yourself and discover your true self. We often state that you should treat other people as you would want to be treated yourself and you should apply that principle to yourself as well so you can become your own best friend. Then of course in a relationship there must be chemistry together with that all important bond of friendship. The chemistry will provide the physical attraction and the friendship will enable you to grow together.

Summing up the major points:

- Always treat people as you want to be treated.
- Discuss your problems with your partner – agree to disagree sometimes.
- Prioritise your time - enhance your relationship. Remember the greatest gift you can give is your time.
- Try to understand your partner's or the other person's point of view – even if you disagree.

- Anger and aggression – Be aware of your anger 'triggers' and be prepared to change your behaviour. You should aim to be assertive not aggressive.
- Mix with people whom you admire and who inspire you.
- Strength of Character – is built on the 'downs in life' and not the 'ups;' basically, it is how you cope with your problems under pressure.

10

Look Good, Feel Great – Health

Your Number One priority! Look after yourself! With good health the world could be your oyster.

It is such a great pity that so many people take little or indeed no exercise at all. Not only does it make you feel so much better but the overall health benefits are enormous.

The secret is simple. Make exercise as interesting as possible for yourself. Write down all the ways of taking exercise that you can think of and then look at the list to see which appeals to you. Most people like to walk a little or occasionally to run. Cycling is normally a favourite or playing some form of sport with the children can be fun. Simple exercise can be achieved at home whenever the time permits.

All your time spent exercising is cumulative, however simple it may be. Even breathing and posture exercises count towards the totals. Once the initiative is in place the habit will grow and daily exercise will become a normal routine. Keep a record of your activities because it will help to motivate you and spur you on. The fact that you will feel fitter and perhaps begin to lose a little weight will be a massive incentive. Above all, remember that achieving healthy exercise can really be great fun.

Joining a social and fitness centre can be a family or group project. A whole family or perhaps a group of work colleagues can join together, socialise and achieve their individual fitness targets together. You will really enjoy using the club facilities and feel so much better when you arrive back home. Get together with friends, family or work colleagues and plan group activities because it really is a great way to socialise.

When you think about your overall personal fitness, exercise and diet go hand-in-hand. When considering your options exactly the same principal applies to diet as well as exercise. You must make it as interesting as possible. Write down all the food that you enjoy and you may be surprised to see some good wholesome, non fattening items listed. Most people like some vegetables, salads, less fattening soups, jacket potatoes, lean meats, fish and fruits. It is rare for example to find people who don't like bananas, melons or oranges. Combined with normal sensible eating many of these items can ensure a balanced healthy diet.

Health, diet and exercise is normally a personal consideration, but in some professions it is mandatory. David remembers the time when he was aircrew and flying worldwide sorties. We flew endless hours in varying time zones and differing climates. Maintaining a healthy diet and keeping fit was very difficult. We had to undergo a regular strict aircrew medical which included body weight and general fitness. Eventually after much frustration I used the body clock as my regulator. Regardless of the time and location when I awoke I would eat breakfast and at the end of my working day I would enjoy an evening meal or its equivalent, relax and then sleep. A very definite compromise but it worked for me despite the looks people give you at 7.00am in the morning when you have just been enjoying an evening meal, have a cup of cocoa and are dressed for bed.

So if you have a problem because you are working shift or unusual hours try using the body clock yourself. Basically, your day starts when you get up regardless of the actual local time on your clock. It finishes when you are ready to go to bed.

The way we look after ourselves and our personal health and fitness also has serious connotations in the workplace. Work-related stress is now responsible for more absentee-ism than any other cause. Generally people are working much longer hours to achieve unrealistic targets and the threat of multiple redundancies is now a common work place fear. There are an estimated eight million working days lost to stress related illness every year. Due to the enormity of the problem, companies, both large and small, should now be realistic and encourage their work staff to participate in employment- sponsored exercise and relaxation schemes. Corporate membership of fitness centres and health spas should be increased and employers must actively encourage their employees to join the schemes as well as private clubs. Companies have to realise that if an employee is reasonably fit, enjoys a well balanced diet, is well motivated and employed in a positive but stress free working environment it will create a definite overall increase in company productivity.

As well as exercise and relaxation, humour in the workplace provides an excellent stress release. It relaxes people and lifts their spirits, boosting their body chemistry. Laughter, in particular, is infectious. It tends to resonate around an office, improving the overall atmosphere and creating a sense of well motivated staff contentment.

Jean believes that we must all ask ourselves the question: what does being fit mean to you? Does just being able to walk upstairs without getting out of breath mean you're fit, or is running a marathon your idea of fitness. Well of course there are all the levels in between, but we all know that to be healthy we do need to have a certain amount of fitness. It's a fact that at the beginning of each year there is a huge increase in gym memberships but by the end of February a lot of people have fallen by the wayside. There is no point in spending a lot of money joining a fitness club unless you know you will really love the whole experience of working out in a club environment.

There are many other ways of keeping fit. For example, using the stairs instead of the lift or taking the dog for a walk. Of course you can always walk someone else's dog for them if you don't have one of your own. You could try a dance class if it appeals to you more than an aerobics session and it will do you just as much good. Become imaginative and see how many ways you can think of keeping fit, then try each one until you find the one you like the best. You will maintain your interest for longer if you really enjoy what you are doing. This way you will want to make it a part of your life and not see it as a chore. Provided that you maintain your positive attitude it will help you to keep fit and healthy for the rest of your life.

I believe that visualisation and positive thinking are very important for achieving and maintaining good health, Jean states. My father always said and taught us as children that mind over matter cured most things. I believe he was one hundred percent right. He had a massive heart attack at the age of fifty two and then years later had a burst aorta, but he lived for many more years to the astonishment of all the doctors. He always saw himself as fit and well and lived his life that way.

I feel strongly that we cannot separate our physical health from our mental, emotional and even our spiritual states of being. This means that our illnesses or diseases that we hold in our body can possibly stem from something that happened in our lives, even as far back as our childhood. We must learn to listen to what our body says to us. In some cases positive instead of negative thinking can change us from feeling unwell to feeling good, hence the saying it's all in the mind. I am not saying that this is always the case, but I am convinced that we can improve our health in many cases. We must learn to dismiss the past because it's over and live in the here and now. Some illness stems from repressed feelings and we may need outside help or support which may be found through a therapist, healer or maybe just a good friend to talk to.

It is also important that we all take time to relax and the way that we do this is different for everyone. Some people find that exercise helps them whereas others find just lazing about watching television is relaxing. There are those who like to meditate or do Yoga or Pilates. The thing to remember is that we should never criticise or mock others for the way they choose to relax. The whole idea is just to do what is right for you. For men it may be a game of golf or just pottering around in their garden shed. For me it is swimming or just sitting in the Jacuzzi and I must admit that this is also the time when my brain seems to do all it's thinking. I seem to get all my best ideas in the Jacuzzi when I am really relaxed. If I totally want to switch off then it has to be a good film on TV. Just do what is right for you because relaxing is so important for your health.

I also think that you have to have a belief system that supports you, and again this may be different for all of us. It may be religious but it can be whatever you choose. For me it is meditation and using Reiki which is one of the fastest growing healing therapies.

The Reiki principles are:

Just for today do not anger.
Just for today do not worry.
Honour your parents, teachers and elders.
Earn your living honestly.
Show gratitude to every living thing.

I also believe in listening to my intuition. I find that if I relax and close my eyes I can then ask for the answer to a particular question. I trust that the answer will come to me through my subconscious and it usually does.

I can't prove that Reiki or whatever you believe in really works. Neither can I prove that praying, asking the universe or whatever you believe in will work. What I do know however is that I believe it works for me. It works as a spiritual support for all the practical and not so practical things that I choose to do in my life, especially when things are difficult. Basically it makes me feel more positive and much healthier.

Without a positive attitude, I certainly would not have been so successful in my professional life. I always believed that I was good at what I did, and that I deserved to do well. I truly believed that I would be successful, and that I would succeed. I also know that we have to set ourselves goals and see opportunities whenever they show themselves. To achieve those goals we must remain fit in mind and body.

You need to forget the 'old' way of thinking which has stopped you from moving forwards and say thank you every day for your blessings. Start a completely new way of thinking that will rid you of your insecurities and let you move on to the life you choose so that you can be just what you want to be.

Try being as positive as you possibly can be. Tell yourself that you will achieve your aims and try to really believe in your ability to succeed. If for some reason you don't achieve it today, learn from your mistakes and tell yourself that tomorrow is the day it will happen. You will actually be amazed at the difference in yourself and how you feel about your abilities and your general wellbeing.

We talk a lot about confidence, image and self motivation when referring to people and life skills. Similarly when you set and achieve your sensible fitness targets, you feel so much better. It installs inner and outer confidence in you due to the fact that you feel good and look good. Because you are trimmer your clothes fit better and when people pass compliments about your appearance then you know that your overall image is improving. For some people the controlled loss of weight can be like starting a new life and of course it is so much healthier. The secret is to maintain the balance of the new fitness regime and not to digress into old habits. You must remember when you set out on a life changing project that is just what it is! For Life! Basically it means a total change in your life style which includes new fitness regimes together with a new sensible diet. Realistically it is down to your own personal self motivation.

Throughout my somewhat long journey through the University of Life I have learned and formed opinions on many things, one of them being the subject of weight gain. I am one of the lucky ones who has never been drastically overweight, but there have been periods of my life when I have been carrying more weight than I was comfortable with, so I decided to look into the reason why.

There are normally two reasons for being overweight. Either, eating the wrong type of food or eating too much food. Standard dietary advice will usually include a total change of individual eating habits with regard to both intake and the type of food you should eat.

There is a problem because, despite our list of interesting dietary foods in the opening paragraphs of this chapter, generally typically formal diet-food is hardly inspiring. It can be bland and boring and that is one of the main reasons why many people fail with regard to their attempts at diet planning. The result is that the old problem of weight increase re-occurs time and time again. Some people spend half their lives returning to attempt yet another diet plan! Then again if you are successful how do you maintain your target weight when you have achieved your weight loss? As David always points out, it is realistically down to your own personal motivation otherwise you can become the human equivalent of an elastic band. There is an alternative you may wish to consider however.

My secret is that you should eat like a naturally slim person. They eat only when hungry, just the way a baby does. A baby will refuse food if it's not hungry, it will stop when it's had enough and will only eat what it enjoys eating. We have all seen a baby spit out food it doesn't like.

When you are hungry eat sensibly but try to eat exactly what you want. The question is, how do you know what you really want? Ask your body what it wants. Ask yourself do you want something sweet or something savoury, do you want spicy or bland, crunchy or smooth, then say to yourself what would satisfy your need? If you are eating out look at the menu and see which things you really want. Don't look for the least fattening or the cheapest because the thing that jumps out at you from the menu is usually what you really want and need. If you don't choose what you really need, you will probably go home later and eat more food just to satisfy that need and consequently you will have eaten too much. Basically you need to eat just enough food to satisfy your body's requirements without the intake of unnecessary and excessive calories.

Always eat with awareness, smell it, look at it, keep it in your mouth for a few seconds before chewing. When you have finished ask yourself what feeling does the after taste give you? Eat slowly and completely empty your mouth before the next bite. If you are alone try closing your eyes whilst chewing and see how it makes you feel. Don't do anything else whilst eating such as reading or watching television, because you want your food to be emotionally rewarding as well as physically satisfying. When you have your meal in front of you, try tasting a little bit of each item then decide which you like the best, and start with the most delicious bits. You will consume fewer calories if you get into the habit of eating this way because you will not mind leaving the bits that you weren't so keen on once you are satisfied.

Also remember that when you eat out you are not just paying for the amount of food on your plate. You are paying for the whole experience, the ambience, the music and the company, so enjoy it all.

Another good tip is to have a little food with you all the time. This way you never get to the stage where you are so hungry that you dash into the nearest shop and just buy anything.

If you only eat to satisfaction rather than eating until you are full, you will never overeat or become overweight again. How do you know when you have overeaten? I believe it is when you can actually feel the food in your stomach and if you can feel it then you are full rather than satisfied. You wouldn't overfill your car with petrol but we can overfill our bodies. This fuel then just goes into storage and becomes fat.

If you learn to eat this way you will be a naturally slim person eating all the food you really love and never having to diet again. It is really a matter of eating sensibly and using your common sense. This is the easiest way to becoming the size you are meant to be naturally. The thing to do is listen and feel what your body is telling you.

Concentrate on the following points:

- Exercise - consider all the possible options for keeping fit.
- Make exercise as interesting as possible for yourself - try to enjoy it.
- Try to make keeping fit a social occasion - join in with groups and exercise with friends and family.
- Diet - eat sensibly.
- Working odd hours - use the body clock.
- Corporate value of Health and Fitness - a fit workforce is a good, happy and productive workforce.
- Relaxation - discover your own system and reduce your stress.

11

Getting it Right – Etiquette

The correct and appropriate way to do things. There is a right way and a wrong way. Your credibility is at stake!

You may be surprised to see a chapter about etiquette in a personal development book. We talk about first impressions being very important therefore it is imperative that we make every effort to make sure that we make a dynamic but very correct impact on other people, especially at the first meeting.

Someone once said that the Americans have got it right. They use good manners to make people feel good whilst the British use etiquette and manners to make people feel bad, because of class. Whatever you believe, if we are planning to improve our lives then we should also learn the correct way to do things and that includes general politeness, good manners and the correct protocol.

When I was a child my mother used to say that 'proper etiquette is essential' David recalls. She was a great believer in politeness, good manners and doing things the right way. I was taught to open doors for ladies, give up my seat for older people and always be respectful to others.

One of my mother's favourite sayings was that 'good manners maketh the man.' She was of course absolutely right but we all had to laugh at an amusing true story when, on my first journey to London, I tried to help an old lady off the train with her suitcase. The old lady hit me over the head with her umbrella and told me in no uncertain terms to go away otherwise she would call the police. She was obviously convinced I was a scoundrel who was determined to rob her. My mother thought it was hilarious when I told her. That was the day I realised the importance of making a proper first impression. Eventually the old lady did apologise when she realised my true intentions and I helped her safely off the train with her luggage.

Throughout this book we continually reiterate the need to improve and nurture your people and life skills to create the life you want. At some point in your life when you finally achieve your goals you will almost certainly be mixing with management or successful people. Therefore it is so important that your first point of contact in person or on the telephone gives the correct impression.

The correct telephone etiquette is important and the initial conversation on the telephone with a client should be handled in exactly the same way as any introductory meeting. Remember this is a first point of contact so you must establish rapport and install credibility. Introduce yourself properly, maintain your decorum throughout the conversation and always smile because it does come across to the listener. If you are in doubt about the quality of your telephone voice, try a little experiment. Leave a message on your answer phone and ring yourself up. Again we advise you to practise your telephone manner as often as possible. Ask your friends and family for their opinions of your telephone voice and manner. If you are not convinced, think about the times you have made business calls to companies for the first time. How many times were you impressed with their response and how many times were you not impressed? Now ask yourself why? Good telephone manner and etiquette is essential and there is no excuse for poor telephone manner or etiquette, especially in the business environment.

If you are working from home there are some obvious pitfalls. For example who has access to your telephone? Business clients do not need young children answering their calls. Make sure that you have an answer phone and that it is activated. Your messages on the answer phone must be positive, informative and inviting so that the client or prospective client will be tempted to leave a message, including a contact number. Business clients arriving at your home need to be invited into a clean, uncluttered and tidy area. Animals need to be shut away in other rooms. You visitor does not need your pet Airedale to throw its dirty paws onto their shoulders, lick their face and bury its nose into their ear. This message is clear: do not mix children or animals with business.

So, if you are working from home, use the guidelines above to check your office environment. Most importantly ring yourself up on the telephone and listen carefully to your answer phone. As well as checking the clarity and tone of the message ask yourself if the message conveys the information that you want it to in a professional manner because it can be that all-important first point of contact. Also if business clients come to your 'home office,' make certain it is clean and tidy because first impressions do not stop at the front door! It should look professional not domestic.

Introducing people is one of the most important aspects of daily business and networking activities. You need to remember proper introductions can create long- lasting impressions. By making proper introductions it will free you to concentrate on making a good impression yourself. Always introduce people because if you don't it will be noticed. If you are like us and have difficulty remembering names then you have to find your own system that works for you. When meeting someone for the first time, try saying their name several times to lock it in your memory and hopefully that will help you memorise the name. We discuss memory aides in another chapter but if all else fails then you have to very politely ask for their name again.

When you are introducing people and also when ladies enter the room, always remember to stand up and, as far as the pecking order etiquette is concerned, you always introduce a 'junior to a senior' and 'a younger person to an older person.'

A handshake is the physical greeting. You will be judged by

your handshake and it needs to be firm and confident not limp. The message you should portray is that you are open, friendly and ready to do business.

Recently one of the lady students wanted to know what is the correct and appropriate etiquette for a lady's formal business greeting now that there are more ladies in corporate career environments and running their own businesses

Jean is a business lady and also thinks that handshaking is the most important formal greeting for women. Handshakes are the physical greeting which combines with your words, she says. You are judged on your handshake far more than you may realise and we unconsciously judge others by the way they shake our hand in response. This applies to women as much as to men. The handshake reveals so much about your feelings and motivations. Jean also agrees that a handshake needs to be firm and confident. 'Wimpish' handshakes are not acceptable from men or women, either socially or in business.

The problem from a women's point of view is that boys will have been taught the art of manly handshakes from an early age by their fathers but the chances are that the women will not have been taught at all. A hug is not the best formal corporate greeting unless you are in a Latin country. In my opinion that is why we get more poor handshakes from women than men.

There is still a lot of confusion regarding women and handshaking. Some people are uncertain what to do in a formal greeting and some women are offended if you do not offer them a handshake. Our solution is to take the lead. For a man, if the situation exists where good manners and correct protocol demands a formal introduction, then offer the lady your hand for a handshake. Remember this is the decade of communication so lead by example because humans imitate by nature and if you show positive behaviour others will doubtless follow. The lady will appreciate your gesture and it will enable her to relax. You will then have shown impeccable manners and established excellent business rapport. For a woman, you can of course also lead by example in a situation where formal introductions are being made. Hold out your own hand and there will be no confusion as to whether or not a handshake is appropriate.

The best way to initiate a formal handshake is to put your right hand out flat for a second as a signal. Basically it makes a statement. I am friendly, open and ready for a handshake. You will find that it works for everyone. The next time you meet as one to one or in a group of people follow our advice and practise your handshaking. When you shake a lady's hand, try to gauge her reaction. You will find that most women consider it a compliment. We also urge you all to teach your children to shake hands properly. It will help their own confidence and of course it will enhance other people's opinion of them later in life.

Office etiquette is also very important There are quite obviously dos and do nots in the normal office working environment. Offices can be like families and they are quite often dysfunctional. There are the mother and father figures who think they are always right and know all the answers. Then of course there are the quiet ones, the rebels and the mavericks. In the office environment there is an office work model. In order to score points never be late, do not overrun your breaks, leave your domestic problems at home and keep private calls to an absolute essential minimum. Popularity counts so a few pleasantries will keep you on side with your colleagues but idle gossip is not acceptable. If you are not well stay at home if possible but if you go to work do not play the martyr and complain. Avoid rebellious behaviour because it can alienate you.

Most importantly, dress up to your ambitions. Remember IQ loses impact if you don't look professional. Seductive dressing however is very counter productive. You will not be taken seriously and you could make yourself a target for harassment. If you are in doubt about what to wear, watch other staff and dress as befits your position and role in the company.

A word of warning: mixing business with pleasure needs to be handled carefully. There can be many pitfalls at in house social events. Unchecked alcohol consumption can also lead to the wrong type of conversation and behaviour.

Officers in the Armed Forces are expected to display excellent personal qualities and proper etiquette at all times. Mess functions are steeped in tradition and etiquette. The Friday evening happy hour however is a time to relax and it took me considerable time to get used to sitting next to a padre on the one side of the bar and my doctor on the other David recalls. Whenever I attended church and heard a sermon on the 'demon of drink' I always had to raise a wry smile. Equally funny was the annual aircrew medical when my doctor would ask me if I drank alcohol. I always felt like saying 'yes, it's your round next and put me down as having a good sense of humour.'

One question we are frequently asked is that if we are not certain about the correct etiquette in any given situation what advice would we give? Our answer is that it is obviously not possible to list every circumstance and give an appropriate procedure. Our teaching in all circumstances however, regardless of protocol and etiquette, is to use your common sense. Always ask yourself if you are displaying impeccable behaviour and good manners. Your people and life skills will be instinctive.

Coaching points:

- First Impressions - it is vital to get it right. Make a dynamic but correct impact.
- Working from home - avoid the obvious pitfalls. If your home is your office then 'office rules apply.'
- Introducing people - make proper introductions and establish rapport.
- Corporate greetings - use the correct formal handshakes. Firm and confident not limp!

- Office etiquette - obey the rules and observe the 'dos and do nots' of office etiquette.
- Business and Pleasure - mix business and pleasure with caution.

12

Your Chance to Dazzle
– Formal Occasions

With your knowledge of the correct etiquette this is your opportunity to really dress up and attend up-market functions with ease and confidence.

Imagine the scene. The music drifts down from the minstrel's gallery to add to the relaxed general ambience of the occasion. The candlelight flickers as the silver service serving staff await the signal to move forward to remove the first course crockery and prepare the tables to receive the main courses. Jean and David are attending the Officers Mess Ladies guest night. Although she has attended many different formal occasions Jean has never actually been to a formal Ladies dining in night before and is loving every minute of it. She is enjoying the pageantry and of course the dressing for the occasion as befits her profession. Good food and wine in excellent company, what more can you want. Although it is a formal evening, it is, as many such occasions are, very relaxed.

You could be forgiven for thinking what on earth has a function like that got to do with me and would I ever want the opportunity to attend such an occasion? Well, as your life skills improve and your career progresses, you will almost certainly have to consider attending a formal function of some type or other and the aim of this chapter is to prepare you for such an event.

You may also think that a lot of people would say that they would not enjoy attending formal occasions but just look at the evidence to the contrary. School proms have never been so popular with young school leavers who obviously enjoy the dressing up and the formality. Cruising holidays are extremely popular and most of the passengers simply wallow in the formality. That is one of the reasons they return year after year. The Captain's cocktail party, the silver service dining and the champagne waterfall attracts all the passengers, young and old. Even the lavish afternoon 'English Tea' on board attracts large numbers of semi-formal diners. One of the main reasons why cruising is so popular is because you can combine the formal and casual occasions while travelling to exotic destinations.

It is exactly the same with the theatre and quality restaurants. The simple truth is that many people like to dress up and attend formal and semi formal functions. It is almost a mark of success in life and this is why it is essential that we all have the skills to be able to identify and cope with formal occasions if we wish to progress in life.

Not convinced? Well imagine that you are invited to a wedding in the near future. What are you going to wear? How will you conduct yourself? You may be the best man or a relative of the bride or groom and be expected to stand up and deliver a speech. A wedding is after all usually a formal function. is it not, and people often take a great delight in all the formality, pomp and ceremony. Vast sums of money are spent these days on such occasions and the formal dining arrangements are extremely enjoyable. Just think, you may even be asked to wear a top hat and tails! Graduation ceremonies, speech days and funerals are also just some of the every day formal functions that we can expect to have to cope with as our lives progress.

With regards to success in business, self employment or career enhancement, as our people and life skills improve and develop, it is essential that we realise how important such formal occasions can be to our natural career progression. Just like the correct etiquette and protocol, we must learn the 'rules' of each particular situation. Like all learning environments, the preparation and planning for the big event is paramount.

The first consideration is dress for the formal occasion. For men we recommend they own at least a dinner jacket and a blazer or smart semi formal jacket. David remembers that when he started cruising holidays, he actually decided to buy a 'cruise kit'. He went to a large outlet shopping centre, bought everything at once and actually managed to buy a dinner jacket, a white formal jacket and a really smart jacket for a very reasonable price. Each item of clothing had a pedigree label and David felt that he had purchased real value for money. His cruising kit now doubles for any formal function that he is likely to attend.

There is no substitute for the real McCoy and a good dress shirt and appropriate tie is no exception. Again if you purchase from outlet stores they are a reasonable price. They don't have to be designer labels but simply good quality clothes. Our advice is to buy two shirts because you just know what will happen if you only own one. Red wine can really stain! Finally the shoes and socks: you must make sure that they are appropriate for the occasion, fashionable and the right colour. You may not spend all evening looking down at your shoes but somebody else will check them. If your overall appearance is not right, it will be noticed and noted. If you are considered to be managerial material, and we sincerely hope that most of you will fall into that category at some stage in your career, then our advice is very important.

Formal clothes don't have to break the bank and, as we have already stated, it doesn't necessarily mean having to buy designer labels. The sales are a great time to buy your attire. Ladies evening and cocktail dresses are especially good value in January when the shops are selling off their Christmas stock.

Jean recommends that ladies have a 'capsule' wardrobe which consists of items that are suitable for all occasions. That way, whenever you receive an invitation, you will always have the appropriate clothes to wear and not have to dash out at the last minute to find something suitable. This will prevent you making avoidable expensive mistakes. For those one off formal occasions, another option of course is to hire the clothes.

Now look in your own wardrobe and ask yourself what you would wear if you received an immediate invitation to a formal or semi formal function. If you have a problem answering that question then follow our recommended guidelines.

We have already discussed etiquette skills and of course appropriate methods of greetings and introductions. Your networking skills will obviously help you to socialise in the formal environment and always attempt to establish rapport which will help everyone to relax and socialise.

One excellent tip for men is to learn to dance. There are more and more ladies now managing and running a business, so being able to dance means that you can hold a social and business audience in a congenial atmosphere. The same advice also applies to the ladies of course. Learning to dance can be great fun and a great way to network yourself.

Importantly, formal and wedding invitations will specify dress codes. Usually the invite will state the men's dress code and the women's dress code can be worked out from that. Decoding the dress codes is straightforward enough.

For example, put in simplistic terms:

1. Casual - if the invite states smart casual it does mean please make an effort.
2. Lounge Suit - means a day suit or business suit with a good shirt and tie.
3. Cocktail - means dressy but not evening dress. Ladies Cocktail dresses are usually knee or calf length.
4. Black Tie /Formal - means a dinner jacket for men and a long dress for ladies.
5. Morning Coat / Dress - this is much more formal attire and usually worn at weddings or possibly attending the races. Men will be in tails and ladies in formal dresses, hats and gloves. If the event is after 5pm it could mean that the event has a white tie dress code.

6. White Tie - the ultimate really glamorous, glittery evening event. Men will wear the traditional black dress suit, white tie and black patent shoes. Because these events are considered to be ultra formal, ladies can pull out all the stops and wear their most beautiful gowns.

When circumstances permit, you must take every opportunity to attend such occasions. If you follow our advice then you will almost certainly enjoy the experience and with practice you will begin to look forward to attending formal functions.

Remember, follow the code:

- The Formal Occasion – possibly an important stepping stone to achieve your personal and business aspirations.
- Etiquette skills – essential when attending formal occasions.
- Dressing up – everyone enjoys dressing up on occasions. Imagine attending a wedding or a formal celebration in casual clothes!
- Dress Codes – formal occasions have strict dress codes.
- Buying your clothes – the sales are a good time to buy your formal attire.
- Learn to dance – it's fun, good exercise and a major bonus to enable you to enhance your personal and business networking.

13

Dealing with the Unexpected
– Life Changes

The ability to cope with and, when possible, enjoy those major ups and downs in life.

This is a book about personal development which is a subject that affects us all throughout our lives, young and old. Your strength of character, in particular, is one of the most important aspects of your make up. It is an essential life skill which is particularly relevant during those sometimes traumatic life changes. The aim of this chapter is to help you, the reader, consider your options and help you to cope in life changing situations and circumstances, especially when confronted with difficult personal problems and with regard to retirement issues.

Certain events in life can change your whole life drastically. Redundancy, leaving school, changing jobs, getting married, having children, getting divorced, ill health, bereavement and grief are just a few examples. There are many times when your life and indeed your whole style of life can change overnight, sometimes without any warning. As individuals, Jean and I have both been through many of these major changes and although we are not experts we can at least advise how to cope with the some of these different situations, explains David.

If you can cope with and survive difficult situations in your life you will most certainly become a stronger person in the end. Try to remember that there are probably literally hundreds of people trying to cope with a similar situation at the same time so you are not alone. Always seek advice, surround yourself with friends and family and do not bottle up your problems. Constantly remind yourself that you can and are coping and that the future will be bright. As always, set yourself aims and objectives, especially in the difficult times. Ask yourself what makes you happy and set out to achieve it. You will be surprised because with a positive aim you are so busy you can even forget your problems at times. Never ever give up on your dreams. If you fail to achieve a goal, use it as a stepping stone. Ask yourself why you failed, learn from it and use it to succeed next time. Take great delight in getting to grips with and then solving the problem. If it becomes impossible to achieve that particular goal then simply try a different way.

One of the most traumatic situations is coping with close personal relationship problems. With the best will in the world and despite every effort to the contrary, even the best relationships can deteriorate and even break up. We must ask ourselves the question just how do we use our life skills to cope in these circumstances, especially with all the other pressures in life? Obviously it is a very emotional, as well as a traumatic time, and handling these situations takes a great strength of character.

If you are in that situation, our advice is that the first thing you must realise is that your overall strength of character is built on the downs in life rather than the ups. Constantly tell yourself that when you emerge from the trauma of a relationship ending you will be much more resilient. You must remain positive through the experience and move on. Remind yourself that there is a life out there and go out and find it. Never forget that there are so many people in exactly the same situation so do not wallow in self pity. Create new life styles and meet new friends. Surround yourself with nice people and above all have fun. By creating this new lifestyle you are also creating a different life from the previous one and therefore becoming independent. This will be your cornerstone to a successful new life. Do not use the words "we used to do that" but now say "I am doing" and make sure you smile when you say it! Before you know it you will be really smiling and guess what? You will soon be forming new relationships as the new you. Obviously the advice we give relates to the individual and personal character issues. If there are other issues with regard to children, access, housing and finance we would always advise you to seek professional advice.

Serious illness, bereavement and grief are major problems that each individual person deals with in their own very personal way. This is when your strength of character is really paramount and sometimes it takes a great deal of courage to come through. This is a time when friends and family can help so much and our advice is to talk about your problems as much as possible. We both agree that when we have been in similar situations, close friends and relatives with excellent listening skills can be so helpful. Basically, just talking about a problem can make it seem more manageable. As always, however, if a problem raises professional concerns, such as medical or counselling issues, then you must seek the appropriate professional advice.

As we successfully cope with the traumas in our lives, our strength of character becomes stronger and we create our own benchmarks or life's successful stepping stones. Once created, these benchmarks can be used to put our problems into perspective because, having achieved our benchmarks success-fully, any new problems are purely relative. Basically once you have proved to yourself that you can cope with major problems in life then you have the knowledge that you will always be able to cope.

So, think of the major problems you have overcome in your life and ask yourself how many benchmarks you have created of your own. The next time you encounter a major problem try to use your own life experiences to help you achieve a solution. Remember everything in life is relative!

Not all life changing experiences are sad. Recently we were discussing life changing situations on one of our training courses when a student asked the question how would you cope with a big lottery win? A tongue in cheek question maybe, but for some people it could create major problems. While some people might thrive on the media attention and being in the spotlight, others might not. One answer is not to seek publicity and play for time while you consider your options. Eventually you could explain your change of fortune to people other than those close to you, by announcing that you have received a family inheritance. Psychologically the announcement of such a windfall would probably cause you far less hassle with friends and neighbours than the announcement of a big lottery win and, depending on your circumstances and preferences, possibly enable you to continue living in the same neighbourhood or area.

Points for your consideration:

1. Strength of character – the better you cope the stronger it gets.
2. Benchmarks – life's stepping stones.
3. A problem shared – talk to family and friends.
4. Professional advice – always seek it if appropriate.

Retirement issues can also change your life drastically and most people sensibly discuss their retirement plans throughout their lives. Ask any person in their twenties and they will target an early retirement to live a life of wonderful abandonment in stress free luxury. People in their thirties and forties visualise a more serious future. As they approach their later years the magic words retirement pension suddenly take on a different priority. The majority of people in their fifties begin to worry when they actually do their calculations and realise the stark truth that they simply do not have adequate provision to achieve a comfortable life style in their retirement years. At this stage in life the massive cash boost into the pension fund to provide their required life style in retirement is simply not affordable for them.

Statistics tell us that the vast majority of people never actually provide enough funding to achieve their personal retirement goals. The dissolution of company final salary pension schemes, the roller coaster stock market performances and the ups and downs in the property markets makes forward planning a nightmare. Successive governments have regularly tax raided company pension funds in their annual budget, which has eroded the true value of such funds. State pension and benefit funding has long been linked to indices relating to inflation rather than true cost increases. This has resulted in a slow decline in the real overall value of such benefits.

So what is the solution?

Our advice is that it is never too early to start planning ahead for retirement. Ask yourself some simple questions. Have you made any provision for the future? If not then begin right now. Planning for the future can be exiting and if you get it right you can look forward to a much happier retirement. Retirement is another phase in life so we must apply the same principles as always. We must set our aims and objectives, allocate our priorities accordingly and remain flexible throughout our planning stages.

Our aim is obviously to retire in reasonable comfort with enough finance to fund an active retirement. We can all work out our required financial targets based on our present income and requirements. The earlier in life you start to plan ahead then the better the chances are that you will achieve your goals. The secret is to stay alert and constantly review the situation. Set aside a regular sum from your income, we suggest a percentage, and invest wisely by taking advice from professional experts. Set up a plan, I suggest once a year, to constantly review your forward planning and investments. Seek advice from more than one source and do not be afraid to change direction. Consider your retirement planning as a major project and try to continue to invest in your pension funds because this is ultimately an investment in yourself which can seriously affect your 'life style ' in years to come. Look closely at your mortgage planning to calculate if it is possible to pay off the mortgage prior to your retirement. This would be a real bonus to your overall retirement planning but, as always, take advice from several professional sources. With age legislation relaxing it is now possible to work well into retirement. That may not have been your planning initially but it is possible to add extra funding into your pension funds for late starters. Yet again remain flexible and always consider all your options.

We are not qualified Financial Advisors so we are very careful not to give any formal financial advice. All we can tell you is how we plan ourselves and to date we consider that we have been very successful.

If there is a company pension scheme, remember that if you invest so does the company on your behalf. Add any tax relief you can claim and the advantages add up. Consider tax free financial products and always look around for the very best interest rates available for your savings. Before you invest anywhere, do your research. Even the high street Building Society must remain competitive so search for the best interest rates on offer. If you invest a lump sum in a managed fund, consider the initial setting up and management fees which can of course erode any estimated performance figures. Consider the advantages of drip feeding your lump sum on a monthly basis. This procedure is called 'pound cost averaging' and it takes advantage of the ups and downs of the financial markets. We try never to pay interest charges on bank or credit cards, unless absolutely necessary, by paying them off on time and always take advantage of interest free finance if it is available.

So what about retirement? Is that it? Are you all washed up, not wanted by employers and forced to live out your days in miserable surroundings constantly reminded of your glory days?

Not a bit of it. Retirement is a state of mind, just like life itself. It could be a time of wonderful opportunities to travel, take up new interests, make new friends or simply to relax and really enjoy your new found freedom. There are some remarkable offers on hand for mature people with time to take advantage of and enjoy. In retirement adopt exactly the same principles as always. Set your aims and objectives as usual and be prepared to be flexible as required. Try to adopt a healthy life style with exercise, fitness and a balanced diet. If you live in a large house, consider down sizing. This may allow you more free time, less maintenance and considerably improve your financial position. You may wish to consider possible part time work either as an employee or a volunteer. There are so many new opportunities opening up for experienced, mature people with a life time of important skills.

The high street DIY stores are a prime example. Have you noticed in these outlets how customers usually seek mature advice in preference to the younger staff? Voluntary groups could not survive without retired people to administer and staff their organisations. Even the government allocates priorities to the grey vote as a matter of principle and how right they are to do so. Learn a new skill, improve your knowledge, join a fitness centre, visit long lost friends, take a cruise or write a book. The list is endless. Is this the miserable life style you dreaded when considering life after work? I think not.

So, in a quiet moment, make a list of the all the things you would like to do and achieve when you have the time available. It may be possible that this could be the start of some long term planning because it is never too early to plan ahead in life.

Maybe the answer is a lot simpler. Recently we asked a friend who was about to retire what his immediate plans were on retirement. His reply was that the answer is obvious. "On Mondays I will do what I have always had to do on Saturday mornings. Tuesdays I will do what I have had to do on Saturday afternoons. Wednesdays I will do what I had to do on Sunday mornings and Thursday what I had to do on Sunday afternoons. I will then enjoy a long relaxing weekend for the first time in years."

Jean points out that there can be a big difference between men and women when it comes to retirement planning. Men will possibly have the choice of a company pension fund during their working lives but for women the career gaps to bring up a family or to follow a husband's career moves means that financial and career planning can be much more difficult. In addition the fact that a lot of women run their own small business or work part time to fit in with the demands of the family simply exacerbates the problem. As I see it, she says, we have to have two planning strategies, life change and retirement itself. The two are often linked. My advice is to plan ahead carefully. Consider future finance, possible work in retirement, lifestyle, relationships and health matters.

We should start planning for our retirement long before the due dates, but an awful lot of people don't do this. They are so busy furthering their careers or just earning a living that they think they have no time for hobbies and interests outside their work and family. This is a big mistake. I have met so many people who just can't cope without the routine of their jobs. Men often want to run the house that their wife has been running success-fully for years, or they expect her to do what they want to, now that they are at home every day. They forget that she had her own life and routine before his retirement and of course this may be the other way around for a woman who was the main bread winner.

One of the things worth considering is to find something that you enjoy which is totally different to the sort of thing you did in your working career. I know a gentleman who worked in the corporate world of high technology, yet when he retired he went to a pottery class, discovered he was very good and thoroughly enjoyed it. He now sells his pots and works of art in many galleries. Another also worked in a very male environment and is probably the most macho man I have ever met, but by watching his partner flower arranging one day he decided he'd like to try.

He turned out to be very artistic and made beautiful displays.

Remember we all have two sides to our personalities and it is great fun to discover the side that may have been hidden for years. We need to honour both the 'yin' and the 'yang' sides of our personalities in our individual character make ups. The 'yin' and 'yang' are the overall balance of masculine and feminine traits in a person's character and you can actually work out your own balance, which of course helps you understand so much more about the real you. Basically, 'yin' and 'yang' are the terms used to describe the various facets of our personality. We all posses both male and female traits in our make up; as an example the 'yin' or the female side relates to our creativity and intuition, and the male or 'yang' relates to the technical or more assertive and directional side. Understanding ourselves enables us to know who we really are and therefore present a balanced picture to the world. We are then able to accept and deal with change in a positive manner and it also enables other people to see and understand us better.

My very good friend Margaret, who lectured in the subject of retirement and ran successful training courses in Kent, says that retirement has changed drastically over the last few years, as the one job in a lifetime gives way to the portmanteau career with changing jobs and employment options. However retirement from a lifetime of employment still exists, mid life brings work changes which in their turn bring life changes.

So to summarise, ask yourself what does change or retirement mean to you? Does it mean the end of the road, a feeling of not being wanted or needed any more, nothing seems to matter, it's too late for you now, life is over? Or does it mean an exciting change of direction, a great new challenge, wonderful opportunities, a chance to try something different and more time for yourself?

Be prepared; the following is a list of some of the more important points you should consider:

Finance:

- Save as much as possible into your pension fund on a regular basis.
- If part of the pension is a lump sum, get proper advice on how to handle it.
- Make a will if you haven't already done so.
- Retirement can save you money in travel, fares and business clothes.
- You may possibly need to combine earning and economising.
- Consider part time work or turning a hobby into a money making project.
- Don't ever say 'I leave all the looking after the money to him or her.'
- People who don't understand money management are vulnerable.

Work, occupation and incentives:

- What are you good at and what are the gaps in the employment market?
- Working in the voluntary sector can lead to paid employment.
- Retirement can give you approximately 2180 extra disposable hours per year.
- Develop new interests or resurrect those that have been on
- Older people say that they only regret the things they haven't done.
- Have a go. Join a society, a club or try adult education.
- Don't go into a decline just because you have retired, and don't feel guilty.
- What I am good at and enjoy doing and what I am not good at and dislike?

- Get relevant advice for any problem: money, work, occupation, and legal matters.
- Think: 'I am (your name)' rather than I am a policeman or a teacher etc.
- Ask people close to you what they think you might enjoy or do well at.

Lifestyle:

- Think three times before you move abroad, to the sea, somewhere smaller.
- Two cars or one car? If only one, then whose?
- Work out new house rules with your partner.

Relationships:

- If you have a partner, a changed timetable may affect your relationship.
- Ask yourself has your work taken priority over your close relationships?
- Question yourself! Have you been horrible, boring, or selfish to live with?
- Spending more time together can be good but risky.
- Be careful, you still need to work at your relationship.

Health:

- Take care of it but don't be neurotic.
- Watch your diet and intake of alcohol and cigarettes.
- Watch your weight, don't become a couch potato.
- Don't neglect symptoms, consult your doctor.

14

Inspiration – Stimulated Creation

The emotion that motivates you to achieve great objectives

You have to ask yourself a question: what is it that inspires you? A person, a location, a film or perhaps a score of music? The list is endless.

Whenever David is asked that question, he also automatically thinks of the word motivation because the two are closely linked.

Inspiration is defined as stimulation of the mind or feelings to activity or creativity. Motivation is defined as giving a reason or inspiration for a course of action or to inspire and encourage someone to do something. These definitions are quite complicated but, put simply, the important question to ask is which comes first the chicken or the egg? Do you inspire someone who is then motivated into a course of action or do you motivate someone who is then subsequently inspired to act? The following examples explain the difference.

Some time ago I was actively looking for a way to raise money for a very important charity. One evening I went into a pub and there was a man playing keyboards in the lounge bar. He was very good and inspired me so much that I was determined to learn to play the instrument myself as a way to raise the funds. It was quite a desperate struggle and at first I found it so difficult that I ignored all the black keys on the keyboard. I was determined however and kept thinking of the evening in the pub because if he could do it so could I! Eventually I managed to achieve a reasonable standard using all the keys and have now raised some money for the charity. The simple truth is that I was inspired that evening which motivated me to achieve my objectives.

This book is the other example. I have been motivated to write about the important subject of people and life skills all my life. It took a chance meeting with Jean however to inspire me into action and I genuinely believe that we have inspired each other throughout this project. Encouragement is a major factor which inspires confidence and during our meetings we have both actively encouraged each others thought processes, especially in the research phases of this book. We aim to achieve the maximum possible in the limited time available through a good allocation of priorities, flexible forward planning and inspired motivation.

Inspiration is a powerful medium and if it is harnessed properly then it becomes a very important life skill. The secret is to recognise when you are being inspired and to know how to make the maximum use of that medium by taking the correct actions.

Think of a time when you were really inspired by a person or an event. Did that motivate you into a course of action and if so, were you successful?

You also have the ability to inspire yourself in certain situations. I remember when I was an air traffic control instructor, one of my students was extremely nervous and this affected his ability to do the job. Without the student knowing, I instructed the pilot of an inbound aircraft to ignore the student's instructions and because the weather was excellent to fly a standard visual approach to land. After the landing, and again following my request, the pilot complimented the student on his control technique. The student, obviously thinking that the pilot was responding to his control instructions was inspired by his own actions and the complimentary remarks. His confidence and work rate immediately increased and he never looked back. He never had an aptitude problem at all, he was just massively under confident. That confidence boost was all he needed. It is so very important not to undermine a person's confidence at any time and especially when they are trying to learn a new skill. Equally important when you are the teacher or instructor is to realise that confidence building, motivating and inspiring holds the key to many peoples success. Always, but always, remember what it was like and how difficult it was for you when you were learning that particular skill. I promise you that it will make you a much better teacher.

So how can you use inspiration to help your own personal development? Above are examples of just how inspiration has actually instigated the achievement of some of my own individual personal goals. Learning to play a musical instrument, raising money for charity, writing a book and achieving professional training goals; not to mention making friends, improving teaching techniques, networking with the musical audience which led to more money raising functions and enabling my air traffic control student to achieve the required standard.

Think of all the things that you have wanted to do but have considered them out of reach because you think you do not have the ability. Our advice is to look for the inspiration which will help to inspire you and motivate you into action. So you want to be a sportsman, a singer or an artist. Go to watch the professionals in action and be inspired to achieve your objectives. Just like personal confidence, if at first you don't succeed than have another go. Remember it is only your pride at stake and just think how proud you will be when you finally succeed in achieving your goals. The more difficult the goal, the greater the final success.

Equally when out of the blue you find yourself inspired by a person, some music, a film or simply an event then recognise the feeling for what it is and try to use the inspiration as a personal motivator. With practice it is amazing what you can achieve.

Jean loves to discuss the subject of inspiration. When I talk of one individual inspiring another individual I feel I am so lucky in my professional life, she states. Because I have the good fortune to work on a one to one basis with clients in all areas of their personal development, be it colour, image, hair, personal or business coaching, I have the training and expertise to help people fulfil their dreams. I have received so many accolades and compliments from my clients over the years and many tell me that I inspire them. Some of my clients have been customers of mine for thirty years. Because it is my normal working environment, I take a personal pride in setting very high standards but do not allow compliments to go to my head. To be perfectly honest I am often inspired by the clients themselves. Nevertheless, I am very proud of my achievements and always strive for perfection in everything I do. Some of my clients come to me feeling a little low and request a make over. To have the ability to completely lift their spirits and make them feel so positive and good about themselves is a wonderful gift. As well as inspiring my clients their complimentary remarks to me always inspires me to achieve even higher standards. It is such a wonderful working environment and I have made so many friends due to my professional abilities.

When somebody asks me what inspires me as a person, I reply that I am usually visually inspired. If I go out and visit a beautiful open garden then when I get home I want to spend time in my own garden to emulate it. In the vast majority of cases I am inspired and then motivated. It is exactly the same with décor, clothes and presentations.

I thoroughly agree with David that you must look for inspiration and recognise it for what it is. Not only will it motivate you into action but will inspire your whole personal development. Whatever you do in your career or in your private life, work hard to achieve the highest possible standards. You must look at every aspect of your personal development and make strident efforts to improve. If you are not receiving accolades for all your efforts then you must ask yourself why not? Make a list of all the main areas of your private and your working life. Be honest with yourself and ask if you could do better in certain areas. Remember, yet again, it is only your pride at stake in an honest appraisal. Have no doubt that eventually your hard work will not go unrewarded and you will in turn be inspired by compliments and career progression.

Coaching tips:

- Inspiration and motivation – magic words.
- Be inspired and in turn inspire other people.
- Always try to achieve the highest possible standards in everything you do.
- Teaching a new skill – always remember how difficult it was for you.

15

Inspired to Take Action – Coaching

Personal Life Coaching enables you to achieve targets and personal goals with the aid of mentoring, allowing you to take control of your life and realise your dreams.

The aim of this chapter is to define life coaching and its individual benefits, to give you a choice and an understanding of your options. You can then choose to practise and use the tools that we provide you with in this book to achieve your dreams or perhaps seek that extra help and mentoring that some of us need from time to time to help us achieve our desired goals.

Life coaching is a modern buzz word, so what is life coaching, what exactly does it do, what are the benefits and will it be suitable for everyone and all age ranges? The best way to start to answer those questions is to study the publicity circulated by the larger life coaching company houses.

Professional life coaching consultants use a myriad of complicated terms to explain their guidance and services. Confidence coaching, financial coaching, goal mapping, life mapping, power persuasion, power pitching, building and sustaining motivation are just a few. Although this terminology may seem to be complicated, many of these terms, when actually broken down into everyday words, are actually identical to some of our straightforward personal development skills that we talk so much about.

To prove our point, a lot of the publicity surrounding the major life coaching professionals is duplicated by different companies in an effort to help, assist and solve some of their clients' problems.

Some of the common issues quoted are:

1. The lack of long term planning.
2. The importance of customer relationships.
3. The issue of a sensible balance between work, life and family.
4. Coaching clients to a superb use of time management.
5. Mastering the art of proper delegation.
6. Traditional goal setting techniques.
7. Helping with personal and professional confidence.
8. Achieving greater credibility, purpose and fulfilment in life and at work.

All fairly complex, but read between the lines and ask yourself where have you seen these issues discussed before? Most of these are precisely the same issues that we have addressed in chapters in this book and on our training courses. So, in effect, we have actually been practising and quoting personal life coaching issues or its equivalent.

Jean is a qualified life coach and it is no surprise that she quotes on her web site "I believe I have been coaching for the last twenty to twenty five years of my professional life without realising that what I was doing naturally, had a name."

So it is not surprising that the basic ideology of our book is that, regardless of your position or circumstances in life, you can achieve the life you want and realise your dreams by constantly seeking to improve and nurturing your people and life skills. There are of course, however, some situations that are so complicated they require extra personal help professionally and we would always advise you to seek that help in extreme circumstances. Also, when seeking complicated business solutions you may possibly require outside help to achieve those professional goals and overall ambitions. Again, you must always seek advice if in doubt.

Good coaches rarely give direct advice to their clients. They ask well guided questions using the correct questioning techniques. This allows the coach and client to seek solutions together in a proper team framework. David remembers using a similar questioning technique as an air traffic control instructor, working in a one to one, live flying environment. It always worked exceptionally well and allowed the students to develop their own thought processes and increase their overall work rate. These question techniques encourage the use of indirect questions and do not give the student a solution but gently guide his or her thought processes. For example, "what is your next course of action?" or "what is your immediate priority?" This prevents simple yes or no answers and allows the student or client to fathom out their own options, finally seeking the correct path to achieve their own goals.

Famous sports stars, singers, actors and so many people at the very top of their professions employ coaches. No serious football or sports team would be without one. These stars have natural expertise and top skills but still they constantly seek to improve and that is why they employ a coach. For exactly the same reason any person attempting to reach for the very summit in his or her chosen business profession or for their own personal development would possibly choose to be coached.

The choice of self-coaching is entirely a personal one. As we have already stated, many people will motivate themselves and draw inspiration by reading our book or other personal development publications. A few people however, may need a hand to hold or a reassuring voice to motivate and inspire them. That is why personal life coaching is conducted on a one to one scenario, either in person or on the telephone. In certain cases the telephone is a much better communications environment. There are no distractions so you can completely concentrate on the task. As with all professions however, if you choose to employ a personal life coach the secret is to find a really good one with a credible qualification.

So, if you decide to seek the help of a personal life coach what can you expect? Jean is just one of many life coaches in this fast growing profession and is well qualified to answer that question. Her definition of coaching is that it enables you to perform at your best through the personal and private assistance of someone who will challenge and guide you to keep growing. In business terms it is described as a solutions focused approach.

Her aim is always to raise the level of personal awareness in her clients so they can fully understand situations in their own personal and business life. She helps them to tune into others in a more effective way and helps them determine and achieve better goals by creating a plan of action. She provides the tools, structure and support for them to accomplish more and be the best that they can be. She also, of course, provides a confidential and independent sounding board; what is said and discussed in confidence remains confidential. Jean always tells her clients that she works in partnership with them to create their ideal life and really encourages them to believe in themselves.

My overall aim is always to be my client's partner for success' she quotes on her web site. I help my clients to become the best they can possibly be by enabling them to unlock their true potential and encourage them to achieve their goals.

Initially, when I take on a client, I ask them to sign a contract agreeing the terms under which I will coach them. I then ask the client to write down information about themselves, their goals, expectations and things they might like to change. Next we talk for an hour either one to one or on the telephone when I explore their values. I encourage them to be really clear about what they want and then draw up a plan of action. After this we speak at appointed times on a weekly basis when specific action and challenges are set for the next session. I always assure my clients that their personal coaching will move them forward fast, easily and effortlessly.

Basically, as a personal life coach, I help my clients to achieve the same aims and objectives that we lay down in our book and that is why I am so proud to be a co-author in this publication. The Jean Sinnett and David Jones motto 'together through inspiration to complete fulfilment' was well chosen. Can you just imagine, as a life coach, the feeling that surges through you when you finally help your client to achieve their personal goals?

So following this advice and guidance you can decide if you need to take advantage of personal life coaching or if you can achieve your aims and objectives in life by using this or other personnel development publications. It doesn't matter what job you do, what status you hold or what your dreams and aspirations are, self coaching or using a personal coach can have a dramatic effect on your achievement process. If you are ever in doubt contact a professional life coach and seek their advice. They will be delighted to discuss it with you. There are professional coaching bodies available to help you make your choice so my advice is to consider your options and choose wisely.

As a personal life coach Jean always assures her clients that:

- I will believe in them totally and demonstrate my belief by taking their aspirations seriously.
- I will encourage them to believe in themselves and nourish their self beliefs so they will grow and flourish.
- I will be non judgemental and guarantee absolute confidentiality.
- I will help them to define a plan of action for achieving their goals and aspirations.
- My eyes will be locked onto their vision, sharing it with them; holding them accountable for the results and keeping them on track.

16

Moving Onwards and Upwards
– the New You

Your make over is complete and you now have the motivation and ambition to move on in life.

Jean and David are seated on a restaurant balcony overlooking a lazy, winding river. It is a beautiful day and the views over the river are quite spectacular.

"You see the things in a totally different landscape from here" said David as he leaned over the balcony and pointed out a duck with her ducklings gliding effortlessly down the river.

"I just love the spring time" replied Jean "everything seems so fresh and clean. It's a new beginning."

"It is exactly the same with our own personal people and life skills" said David as he sat down. "Once you have achieved all your aims and objectives it is effectively a new beginning. You must then ask yourself how best to maximise the potential of the new you."

"Our training programmes are the classic example. We look at each student in the early sessions with regard to their confidence, attitude, motivation, image, dress, style and ambition. We then formulate the best overall individual marketing package for that particular client. Let's face it, we are all marketing ourselves every day whether it is for job search, career enhancement, networking, relationships or personal ambition. You do not necessarily have to do a professional course to establish the way ahead or to find the best formulae for your achievements but it is an excellent way to check your personal progression and ambition."

"To help you achieve your aims it will help if you occasionally return to the basics and recap! You have to define your ambitions and set your goals to achieve them. Practice makes perfect. Take every opportunity to meet people and network. Ask opinions about your dress and image and apply for career moves which will also practise your interview techniques. Listen to the way you project your voice and make a conscious effort to improve your listening skills. Improve your attitude and team working ability. Stand up and talk to people, practise your presentation skills which really can be good fun and regularly step outside your comfort zone. Overall, create the best individual package for yourself and constantly seek to improve it. Never be afraid to fail. Embrace failure and learn from it. Ask yourself where you went wrong and correct your mistakes. It may just be that the competition was too strong. If that is the case, improve yourself to the point where you can compete and win! Never lose faith in yourself and remember you are you and very special. Remind yourself that it is only your pride that is at stake and how proud you will be when you succeed."

"Many years ago a very senior RAF Officer gave me sound advice. Always treat people as you wish to be treated yourself and remember that when another rank salutes a commissioned officer in the armed forces they are actually saluting the hat badge. He pointed out however, that it is always obvious when they actually salute the person themselves, because it is all about personal credibility, leadership and the way you present and conduct yourself. He was so right and it is exactly the same in any given management situation. You have to earn your own credibility!"

"The advantages of the new you are quite remarkable. You will be seen in a completely different light. You will be far more positive, interesting and the sort of person other people will want to meet and be with. You will have that essential leadership quality of 'presence'. When you speak people will listen because you will be authoritative and probably fairly humorous. You will almost certainly notice a daily improvement in your skills. The new you will enhance your quality of life, help your career prospects and improve your personal relationships."

"You have already taken a massive step in the right direction by reading this book. Now, ask yourself that so important question yet again. Would you buy you the package?"

"If the answer is no then turn back to Chapter 1 and recap the journey by setting your own aims and objectives. We always begin with your Personal Confidence."

"Welcome to the campus of the University of Life!"

Jean grinned "I just love a positive ending."

"My message to the readers is that I really hope that now David and I have shared some of our experiences and lessons we have learned during our lifetime, that you will be able to move forward and become the 'you' that you really want to be. I have been fortunate enough to be able to turn my passion into my profession and have had the pleasure of working with so many people in a variety of ways. One of the things I noticed very early on in my coaching practise is that when a person can define their values and beliefs and come to terms with the significant role that these play in forming their own mindset, that is the moment they start to change. The identification of limiting beliefs is often one of the most powerful experiences a person will ever have. Overcoming limiting beliefs can be a light bulb moment for so many people."

"Limiting beliefs are those little voices in your head telling you that you are not capable of doing something. I call them my gremlins because those are the voices that talk incessantly about your limitations. You will never be completely free of these 'saboteurs' but you can control the way that you react to them. You need to recognise the difference between constructive and destructive self talk. When you find yourself resisting or struggling with something it is often a sign that you are listening to your 'gremlins' instead of your positive true voice. You can also victimise and limit yourself by wallowing in the past. Other people may also try to use past references to manipulate you so it is important that you don't live your life now based on earlier beliefs, especially if they are negative and limiting."

"My message is clear. You must reassess your internal vocabulary and check out how many times you use phrases which reflect your limiting beliefs. How many times do you say I should do this, I can't do that, I'm worthless or useless. By changing your speech behaviour you will be changing your attitude in the right direction. Be positive!"

"It really is powerful stuff! For example it is essential that a personal coach identifies and overcomes their own limitations before attempting to coach any one else. As you progress and expand your coaching experience the knowledge that you have left your own limiting beliefs behind gives you the confidence to help others to do the same"

"I really do believe that when you know that you look the best you can, you feel good, you eat well and take good care of yourself. Your confidence also grows as a result and when your confidence levels are high you stand a greater chance of motivating yourself, achieving your dreams and having the life you want."

"My passion is to inspire, challenge and motivate people to take action and create their ideal life. I also believe however that with focus and an effective plan of action you can do it for yourself using the tools that we have set out for you in this book."

"My coaching practice is called 'New You Coaching' and this is not a co-incidence. Now you know why! Good luck to you all."

Jean and David walked slowly over a bridge back to the town centre. They watched as the mother duck and her ducklings now sailed silently towards the distant bend in the river.

"Look at that" said Jean.

"It's so serene and perfect."

"But you can't see all the hard work that goes on under the water to make it look like that."

"It takes a good work rate, confidence, team effort, style and inspiration from the leader to achieve that" David replied with a smile.

"Just like us" Jean grinned.

"You mean hidden depths?" David burst out laughing.

It certainly was a most beautiful day.

Living Your Dream Forever
the Television Series
− Consolidating the Ideology

Living Your Dream Forever the Television Series - Part I

David Jones (02 June 1530pm), 'Morning Television Series', e-mail to Mike Sawyer, Head of Programming, Mid Counties Television.

Dear Mike,

Jean and I were discussing our individual forthcoming commitments during our weekly training meeting here at my house, when we came up with a great idea. Following the launch of our book 'Living Your Dream Forever' through The University of Life, we could front a live 'people and life skills' slot, every week, on your daily early morning programme, We would answer questions from the studio audience and viewers, broadly based on the ideology of the book This show could be an instant hit and help you to achieve those precious target viewing figures of yours. Our book has received plaudits because of the way it has been written and its links to individual personal development. We actually highlight some of the prominent points of view with our own life experiences.

I would suggest either a series of weekly slots dealing with differing topics but with the usual overlap from one week to the next or straight forward question and answer sessions. It would be a light hearted but in depth look at individual personal development with a serious commitment and an essential message to the viewers. As you are aware this is a subject very close to our hearts and something we are passionate about. The topics will range from the way we look to time management and personal relationships to health matters. All very topical subjects, I am sure you will agree. As usual, at present, I am employed using my corporate skills but I would be delighted to find time for such a series. Jean has her diary open just waiting for your call but warns that it is filling up fast! As you yourself Mike have often pointed out, Jean and I make an excellent team with the right balance of fact, humour and opinion. The chemistry is perfect. We could invite a celebrity or guest presenter each week just to counter our opinions and liven the debate.

Mike I hope you are well. Let me know what you think but make it quick before we get snapped up by the opposition.

Regards as always,
David and Jean

Mike Sawyer (04 June 1345pm), 'Morning Television Series,' e-mail to David Jones

Dear David and Jean,

Great to hear from you both. I hear what you say but I have to admit that I have not yet had a chance to read your book. Co-incidentally, the girls at the studio were discussing it at lunch on Thursday after your recent visit here. I have to admit that we desperately need new ideas like a breath of fresh air. As you quite rightly point out, the training and application of individual personal development is extremely topical at the moment.

This weekend my mother in law is visiting so it will give me the perfect excuse to retreat to the study and lock myself away for a few hours to read your book.

David, please e-mail me a copy of the book and I will be in touch as soon as I have read it.

Regards,
Mike

PS: Don't you dare talk to the opposition until I get back to you!

David Jones (04 June 1530pm), 'Morning Television Series', e-mail to Mike Sawyer
Attachment: The book, 'Living Your Dream Forever' through The University of Life.

Hi Mike,

Thanks, I am attaching a copy of the book and hope you like it. I wait with anticipation. Look forward to hearing from you,

David

PS: don't forget to pass the book on to your mother in law when you've finished.

Mike Sawyer (07 June 1130am), 'Morning Television Series', e-mail to David Jones.

Hi David and Jean,

Well, I've read your book despite my weekend house guest. My mother in law always takes over all our weekend arrangements every time she visits so it was great to escape into my study to read. I must say that I think your book is positive, inspirational and to quote yourselves so 'in vogue' at the moment. If you can get that message across to our viewers then we have a deal. I envisage a question and answer session with studio audience, e–mails, texts and phone in. You are right, we should invite an expert or celebrity guest each week to add that extra interest or glamour. I want to set up a meeting with yourselves, Tom the producer of our 'Morning Show' and Adriane our Fashion Consultant, to discuss the finer details.

David, call me on Tuesday, I am in the office all day and we can organise a time and date to get together. I hope you both are not too tied up at present because I would like to action this idea as soon as possible.

Regards,
Mike

Living Your Dream Forever the Television Series - Part 2

Scene: Studio 2 Mid Counties TV

Those present:

> Morning show hosts: Lisa Houston and Graham Bell
> Guest hosts: David Jones and Jean Sinnett
> Guest celebrity and professional expert: Alan Johnson, TV
>   pundit and Managing Director of 'The Elite Fashion House.'
> TV crew and studio audience

8.50am: David and Jean are seated on a three seat couch directly across the studio from Lisa and Graham. Alan Johnson is seated in the single chair nearest the camera crew. The studio audience are already in position and the camera crew are making last minute checks on sound and equipment. An air of 'expectation' hangs in the atmosphere.

"5 minutes!" a voice from the control gallery broke the silence...

"3 minutes, Lisa camera 1" said the voice.

Lisa adjusted her position on the sofa to face the camera.

"2 minutes!"

David looked at Jean and thought that she seemed quite relaxed. He felt nervous and hoped it wouldn't show. After all this was his first time on live television. He had been on the radio several times but of course this was something else.

"1 minute" Lisa smiled at Jean and David as much as to say just take your lead from me. Graham coughed and cleared his throat.

10 seconds, 9, 8...

9.01am: Lisa Houston "Good morning my name is Lisa Houston and together with my co-presenter Graham Bell we welcome you to our daily morning programme on Mid Counties

Television Channel 6. This morning we also welcome David Jones and Jean Sinnett co-authors of 'Living Your Dream Forever' through The University of Life, together with Alan Johnson from 'The Elite House of Fashion' who is the co-presenter on our evening 'With Fashion' programme. For the next five weeks David and Jean will be here with guest presenters to host special question and answer sessions based on the ideology of their book."

Lisa turned to the audience "I've read it and found it extremely interesting. Those of you who haven't read it yet, I recommend you read it! The book is essentially a life guide which promotes the importance of personal 'people and life skills.' The co-author's strong belief is that you the individual can achieve your aspirations and ambitions by constantly striving to nurture and improve your own personal skills. David and Jean acknowledge the fact that few people have the opportunity or ability to achieve high academic qualifications and promote this book and the university of life, as an alternative from which everybody has the ability to graduate. They also make the point that, in this day and age, even if you have achieved the highest academic qualifications your career development will be almost entirely dependant on your personal development and people skills. Companies now want to know what you bring to their doors and what you can achieve for them. A very valid statement!"

"For the next five weeks the audience and you the viewers at home can put that theory to the test by contacting the show and putting your own questions to our guests by calling, texting or e-mailing Lisa.houston@midcounties.co.uk. The contact numbers are now on the screen..."

9.03am Lisa:" Graham, I think you have the first call for us."

Graham: "Michael is on the line and has a question for David."

Michael: "Hi David, first of all can I say that I've got the book and I really enjoyed it."

David. "Thanks that's great to hear, how can we help?"

Michael "David, my real name is not Michael and I have deliberately disguised my location because I don't want my boss to know I am making this call. Tomorrow I have a massive career promotion interview and I need your help. I have been recommended for advancement within the company and with the guidance from your book I have improved my confidence, attitude and general demeanour. I have done a thorough research on my prospective terms, references and responsibilities but basically I still feel a little nervous and under confident about the interview and would like your advice. This promotion means so much to me because it is such a massive step in the right direction."

"Can you help me?"

David: "Michael, if I may call you by that name. You epitomise the type of person that Jean and I wrote this book to help. At the outset of this project we both agreed whole heartedly that we obviously hoped that many people would read, enjoy and above all benefit from the book so I am absolutely delighted that you called me. Listening to your voice I have no doubt that you will be successful tomorrow. Michael it is completely normal to feel apprehensive and you do absolutely right to consider all aspects of the interview but never forget that you are being invited to interview for the post because of your past performance within the company. You would not be attending that interview tomorrow unless your superiors thought that you were the right material so you have every right to feel extremely confident in yourself!"

"My advice is to be punctual, positive and look the part! Know exactly why you are there, why you are the best person for the job and what you can do for the company. Above all Michael, be determined! Give a good firm initial handshake, establish rapport, sit up straight, adopt a positive manner and speak at your normal pace; do not rush your answers."

"An HR friend of mine always states that in any interview situation you must think how you can help the interviewer. Ask yourself what questions you would ask you the candidate if you were in the interviewers chair and you will be amazed how accurate you can be. Listen carefully however, to all the questions you are asked and give a sensible measured response. Stay in control because basically an interview is a two way communication!"

Jean lent forward, "Michael, David is so right, preparation is the key to success. Follow David's advice to motivate yourself and never forget that despite the fact your interview is with your present company, your first impression when you walk in that room is so very important. You must project the right image. You are already working for the company, so, if you have any doubt about what to wear, dress to the standard befitting that particular post."

Alan: "Yes I agree with Jean. Your image is so important Michael. The company obviously know your abilities but you still have to impress the 'hierarchy'. I conduct many such interviews in my company and you will be on show from the moment you step in the room. As David says know exactly why you are there and what you can do for the company. Good luck!"

Michael: "Thank you all very much for your comments. I am so grateful for all your help and advice!"

9.06am: Lisa: "Michael you must let us know how you get on. We all wish you the very best of luck for tomorrow."

"Next we have an e-mail for Jean and David from Mary in Swindon. She says that she has been turned down for jobs several times in the past few months. She has been told that her image is not right and wants to know what she can do about it."

Jean: "Good morning Mary. As you know I am a personal development and image consultant. You will read in the book about first impressions. From a professional point of view I would of course have to see you to give individual advice but as a rule of thumb if the companies are implying, or even that you yourself suspect that your image is the reason that you are being turned down, then it has to be the way you are presenting yourself at the interview. What you need to remember is that the way that you package yourself is of supreme importance. Think of yourself as the goods and your clothes, hair and make up as the wrapping. A good tip for you is to check out the company dress code which they aspire to for the position that you are applying for and dress in a similar fashion. Wear subtle make up and have your hair well groomed. For a more in depth answer look on my web site at www.jeansinnett.co.uk for information on my colour and image consultation."

9.09am: Graham Bell. "The gentleman in the second row, aisle seat, you have a question?"

"James Barrymore, yes, a question for David. Surely you just can't get a decent job these days without academic qualifications. To assume that people skills alone will get you an interview is wrong isn't it?"

David: "Of course you have to have a basic skill to get a job. What we are saying however is that your 'people and life skills' are so important with regard to your career progression. It is the image you portray, the way you behave, your team skills and basic common sense together with your reliability, honesty and overall general impression. We also stress that the highest qualified people have high academic qualifications combined with excellent people and life skills. If however you are not fortunate enough or have not had the opportunity to achieve the academics then concentrate on your people skills; they will take you a long way."

Alan Johnson: "I agree entirely with David! I employ many people in my organisation and I can tell you categorically that I just cannot employ enough people with those skills. I can train my staff to achieve the business objectives I set them but to delegate I need people I can trust as excellent salespeople and administrators. As David points out in the book, the first point of contact for a business is so important; it can make or break a company. I want staff who are willing, polite, have an excellent telephone manner, are competent and also look the part. Above all they must have that old fashioned commodity, common sense!"

9.12am: Lisa Houston. "Linda from Bristol rang to say how much she enjoyed the book. She particularly found the 'time management' section very useful. She says that she created the one hour a day for herself by carefully planning her day in advance and it worked! The only problem is she kept forgetting to go to the supermarket for her cat food."

David grinned.

"Thanks Linda; you obviously need to concentrate on your advance planning, we cannot be cruel to animals."

Lisa: "John from Manchester texted to ask if he practises his golf swing will it help his corporate image?"

"Hello John, the answer is simply yes. If you belong to a golf club you must concentrate on your standards of dress and the image you portray. Given time you will meet the right people for business networking and career progression. As we state in the book so many jobs are not advertised but networked."

Jean: "David is so right. Concentrate on your image and the way you come across to people. Ask family and friends to monitor your progress; tell them what you are doing and why, you will be amazed how helpful they will be. If you have a minute have a look at my web site and see the options you should consider. It will make all the difference to your image."

9.15am: Graham Bell. "Claire from London has a question for Jean."

Claire: "Jean I have recently got divorced! I am fed up and now intend to go for the jackpot. I have no money but I am determined to meet a millionaire and get married. How can I go about it?

Lisa: Wow! at this point we will take the break so don't go away; I am sure we are all waiting for the answer to that particular question Claire. Back soon!"

The morning programme set faded from the big screen at the back of the studio and was replaced by an advert for breakfast cereal. David visibly relaxed and looked at Jean. She was laughing with Alan and Lisa. David thought she looked so much at home in this environment.

The voice from the control gallery broke the silence.

"30 seconds. Lisa Camera 2". Lisa acknowledged by touching her earpiece and turned face the camera.

The big screen at the back of the studio started counting down in unison with the voice. An advert for hair gel faded and was replaced by a sign 'Good Morning' Part 2.

10 seconds, 9, 8, 7...

9.17am:Lisa Houston. "Welcome back everybody."

"As I was saying before the break. Claire is on the line from London. Recently divorced she wants to meet and marry a millionaire. I think that everyone in the audience and at home has been eagerly awaiting your answer to this one Jean!"

Jean stifled a grin "Hi Claire, what an amazing coincidence! A previous client of mine set herself exactly the same goals as you have done. She is now in a serious relationship, is very happy and tells me that they are planning to get married in the near future. Claire if that is a serious statement you need to start looking and behaving like a millionaire's wife now! I suggest that you buy yourself one wonderful outfit of the very best quality you can afford. Dress agencies situated in expensive areas are a great place to find good quality clothes at lower prices. You then need to frequent the places that the 'rich guys' hang out. Think of this as a project and apply the rules that we have set out in the book to achieve your goal. Use our guidelines to check the way you speak and above all think about that all important first impression. You have to look, talk and be the right person.

Remember this is your investment in your future. Good luck and please send me an invite to the wedding."

The sound of laughter from the audience was stifled when Lisa spoke.

9.19am: Lisa. "Thanks Jean and the very best of luck to you Claire."

Lisa smiled "Listen to what Jean has to say Claire. She obviously has the 'Midas' touch and please let us know how you get on!"

Lisa pointed to the audience, "The lady with her hand up, back row. Do you have a question?"

"Yes, my name is Marion and I want to ask about 'speculative letters' to prospective employers when you are looking for a job. Does it really work? Can it help you to find the job that you want?"

David: "Marion, there is no cast iron guarantee in any job search but you must realise that you are 'marketing yourself' in the job market. Once you have satisfied yourself that you have created your perfect personal 'package' then it is time to advertise yourself. Look upon it in the same way as selling any product and basically try everything you can think of; in this case the product is you. The main objective of the 'speculative' letter requesting 'advice' is to get you to meet the recruitment HR person in a particular company. Once granted an advice interview you are in the perfect position to market yourself. Always have an up to date CV with you which you can leave at the interview. If you target several companies and only get one or two results then it has been well worth while. Alan, how do you feel about speculative letters from possible job applicants seeking advice and guidance in your job market environment?"

Alan: "My company policy is that anyone who shows the initiative to write a good letter to my company will always get a reply from my HR department. It shows a positive attitude and I like that. They would have to be suitable in all respects of course but yes I don't envisage any problems in giving that advice. Again, if somebody does stand out from the crowd then they are possibly one for the future; but no guarantees of course!"

Marion: "Thank you that is excellent feedback."

9.22am.Lisa Houston: "David a question from me, how did you two meet?"

David: "Jean and I live in the same neighbourhood and a mutual friend introduced us initially. Several days later I was watering one of my Acer trees over my fence when I heard a shout. Jean was out walking her dog and as she passed my house she got soaked. I rushed out with a towel and apologised; we started talking, became good friends and the concept of our project grew from there."

Lisa laughed and with a sly grin said, "Well, that's novel, no pun intended of course."

Jean: "David talked about wanting to write a book on a subject that was very important to him and I told David about a new training course that I was going on. He was very interested so I also told him about some of the other training courses I had attended and how I had qualified as a trainer myself. He wanted to know more so we decided to meet up and talk. During our meeting he told me that he had always wanted to write a book about 'personnel development' and that our meeting had inspired him to do so. He asked me if I would be his co-author and project co-ordinator."

David: "Jean and I have both got a great sense of humour. As we wrote the chapters we sent each other 'snail mail' by walking around to each others houses with manuscripts in large envelopes. I said to Jean if they ever make a film of the book the people who play our parts will have to spend a large part of the filming walking up and down delivering large brown envelopes. From then on whenever I made a delivery I would grin like a Cheshire cat just thinking about it. The neighbours must have thought I was mad."

Lisa: "Will there be a follow up book?"

Jean: "Most definitely. The subject is endless and so important. People find the subject fascinating and of course it plays such a large part in all of our lives."

David "Lisa, I would just like to say that working with Jean has been great. She is a total professional in every sense of the word and we have had so much fun during the project. She wears several professional hats in her business environment and did me the great honour of wearing another one just to work with me. To find somebody with such similar beliefs as myself and prepared to work jointly on this project was quite amazing. We both passionately believe in the ideology of this book and sincerely hope that it is an inspiration to our readers."

9.25am: Lisa. "I have an e-mail from Lady called Fiona who has a question for Jean. She asks what is your advice to someone who feels stuck in a boring relationship, doesn't have a very interesting job and is generally fed up with the way their life is going?"

Jean: "My answer to that question Fiona is that we always have options. In every predicament you the individual can choose how you are going to deal with the situation and how you yourself feel about it. The important phrase that we must always remember is 'consider all your options,' because it is important to keep an open mind to any new ideas that your previous attitude may have prevented you considering. Wherever you are or whatever the circumstances you can always make the situation better. The main thing is not to become emotionally immobilised. Ensure that you turn the situation into a growing or learning experience and always stay interested in your own wellbeing in order to get the very best out of the experience. You can then make that all important decision to be content with where you are or to work towards a more fulfilling life. Just keep in mind that life is a continuing series of experiences."

Lisa: "Thanks, good advice Jean! We all tend to feel we are in a rut from time to time and of course the solution is always in your own hands."

Jean nodded "and that is why professional coaching can sometimes be invaluable. It can help an individual to develop and 'grow' because, as I said, coaching will possibly enable that person to consider numerous positive options that their attitude may have previously prevented them considering."

9.28am: Graham Bell. "This is one for Jean and probably Alan. Carol has e-mailed and asks Jean if she can work her magic with any lady regardless of age, size and looks?"

Jean: "Absolutely and of course it's exactly the same for men. I don't believe we have to be any particular size or age to look wonderful, we just have to make the very best of what we have. We do this by wearing clothes in colours and styles which suit and flatter us. Pay attention to detail and always look well groomed."

Alan: "I totally agree you do have to make the best of yourself. Sometimes however it pays to consult the experts like Jean regarding suitable colours, styles and fashion. That way you can maximise your potential and save yourself money as well because you will be purchasing the correct clothing to suit you the individual. Watch my 'With Fashion' programme on this channel as well to pick up some really good tips."

"Yes" said Lisa, "you can see Alan's programme 'With Fashion' every week on Tuesday evenings at 8.00pm on this channel!"

9.32 am: Lisa Houston. "The gentleman in the front row with the silver tie, you have a question for Alan and David?"

"My name is Carl Smith and I want to ask you a question David. You state in your book that you always set 'aims and objectives' to establish goals. Is this essential with every task?"

David: "Good morning Carl. Intentionally or unintentionally we always set aims for everything we do. The smaller everyday tasks obviously do not require a formal definition because they are normally single, simple objectives and we do them automatically. When we tackle more complicated time consuming tasks which probably include multi tasking then yes we do need to think ahead, list our aims and the stepping stones we create to achieve our goals. Business projects are a prime example, when several members of staff are involved to achieve a multi tasking scenario possibly combined with different target dates. Individual personal tasks are not so complicated but still require forward planning and a sensible allocation of priorities. Throughout any project, large or small, it is so important to revise your planning because as difficulties arise priorities can change."

David continued "I am often asked by my students for a template to successfully allocate priorities, especially with regard to larger and more important projects. If you do encounter problems selecting and allocating priorities my advice as always is to start at the beginning and list your overall aims. Then write your to do lists and ask yourself the simple question, is each item on the list actually helping you to achieve your overall aim? If not then remove that item from the list. Finally rearrange your remaining list on a time and importance basis. You must obviously do this simple exercise on a regular basis because circumstances change as do the time and importance factors. You will be amazed just how quickly priorities change in any large project and you must ensure that you remain on a direct track of achievement!"

Alan: "I am a great believer in lists! My company projects tend to be rather large and expensive. I consider it mandatory to set aims and objectives and constantly re-assess the priorities as the tasks progress. At present I am supervising a large extension to my clothing Factory. This is an on going project that has been beset with problems since it began due to weather and supply sources. I have to monitor every single stage of the development and re-allocate the overall priorities every week. Yes in business you most certainly have to set aims and objectives as well as ensuring a sensible allocation of priorities."

Carl: "Thank you both for that explanation, it makes a lot of sense."

David "Carl we have a saying in Air Traffic Control that sums it all up. When you are up to your backside in crocodiles, it is difficult to remember that the original aim was to clean the swamp!"

Carl grinned and the whole audience burst out laughing.

"Sounds like morning television" laughed Lisa "we will take a break there but don't go away, back soon!"

The big screen flickered and the studio set faded. The 'adverts' began.

"Well done everybody. 2minutes 53 seconds" said the voice from the control gallery.

Lisa looked at Graham with a satisfied smile. This session was going according to plan and the atmosphere in the studio was extremely positive. Everyone seemed quite relaxed and appeared to be enjoying the programme. Even the director in the control room was smiling, which was most unusual. She nodded her head as much as to say great!

Alan and Jean were deep in conversation.

Graham leaned forward to talk to David.

"I find this whole subject fascinating. In your opinion which of the skills is the most influential?"

"You will be amazed to hear Graham" replied David "but the answer could be humour."

"You see humour is a powerful medium. When used appropriately it relaxes people, establishes 'rapport' quickly, reduces tension, makes introductions much easier and can dilute arguments instantly. The list is endless! In a tense 'one to one' training environment it is a definite aid to relaxation which can create a really positive learning environment."

"It's the same in television" said Graham, "when you walk in the studio or the control room you can always tell a relaxed but professional atmosphere immediately. It's a quietly spoken environment with the odd spate of laughter. When you hear voices being raised it's usually the sign of tension!"

"Precisely" said David "but the humour must be appropriate to the situation and in good taste. I urge caution because we are all different and don't all have the same sense of humour. If you can make people smile then everyone benefits and it is such an asset to add to your people skills. I always look for the humour in life because it makes you feel so much better."

"10 seconds, camera 1 Lisa" announced the voice.

The screen flickered back into action and announced Part 3.

9.37am: Lisa. "Welcome back! Jean here is an interesting e-mail from Kirsty in Slough. She says that she doesn't need advice about her clothes. She wears what she thinks is good for an interview and claims that she has always been successful with every job application."

Jean: "Hello Kirsty. Congratulations with your successes. We try to give advice to the majority of people who do have a problem with making the right choices. Some people however have excellent taste and our advice is purely a validation. Sometimes it is just great to confirm that what you are doing is correct."

David: "Kirsty, Jean is right. We try to help as many people as possible but just like every one else we never stop learning as well. We are two people who have done extremely well in our chosen careers by constantly improving our skills and we try to pass on as much help as we can to other people. We define the skill, describe its importance and then help the reader to try and achieve the ultimate. Occasionally a student on one of our courses has already achieved a high standard on their own so the course is a validation of their efforts and a consolidation exercise. We never forget that we are also on a learning curve and are delighted when we are able to improve our own skills. Kirsty, if ever we can be of any help to you please do not hesitate to e-mail us.

9.41 am. Graham Bell: "Bill from Sheffield is on the line. He has to give a best man speech in three weeks. He is petrified and doesn't know where to start."

David: "Hi Bill can you hear me ok?"

Bill "Yes thank you David. I read your chapter on talks and presentations; you make it sound easy but I am really worried."

David: "Start by just writing down your pleasant memories of the groom and your friends. You must have some good stories to tell. Talk to other people as well because they can often come up with some excellent material. When you have finished write it in a logical order; in time or humour sequence. Now you have the semblance of a speech, draft it out and try it on a friend; often they will help. Once you are happy practise it until you know it backwards and then practise again. Use the mirror and record your voice to hear the play back. It doesn't have to be a long talk just well presented and a little humorous Do not drink very much prior to the speech because it may relax you too much and will possibly slur your speech."

Bill: "Thank you, I will try and keep my fingers crossed! I just can't help feeling very anxious."

David: "Bill, I will tell you what we are going to do. After the show ring Lisa and Graham and they will give you my telephone number. One week before the big day I want you to ring me and practise your speech on me. So Bill you have now got a target. You have two weeks to prepare your speech before you ring me. If necessary I will coach you right up to the day itself. It will be a 'master speech' and will do wonders for your confidence."

David turned to Jean.

"Jean, you give a lot of talks and presentations. From a woman's point of view what advice would you give Bill?"

"My advice Bill is that if you look good you will feel more confident." said Jean. "Try not to speak too quickly as this often happens to people when they are nervous. Keep it fairly short, try to establish eye contact with your audience and remember to smile. Bill following David's tips I am absolutely sure you will be a star and will thoroughly enjoy the experience."

9.44 am: Lisa. "Keith from Warrington is on the line. Keith's question is that in your book you constantly state the importance of personal confidence. Keith asks the question just why is it so important?

David: "Hi Keith, yes just as we said in the book personal confidence is the corner stone of all your people and life skills. There are always times in life when we come to a cross roads in our general life or career progression. Invariably there is an easy route and a difficult route and the latter is usually the way to achieve your objectives in the quickest and most positive way. It takes strong inner confidence in your own abilities however to attempt the difficult route because it is always easier not to make that attempt. That is why I recommend trying to operate outside your comfort zone regularly because every time you do it your overall confidence increases. I can remember when I was in the Royal Air Force having to make a parachute jump. Did I want to jump out of a perfectly serviceable aircraft? No I did not! But you know Keith I summoned up supreme courage and did it! What it actually did, as well as enabling me to go on with my flying course and eventually to achieve my 'wings', was to provide me with a benchmark in my life. Ever since then when I have reached a crossroads in my life I always try to take the difficult route because I know that I have proved in relative terms that I have the confidence to do it! Another thing I do when I reach a difficult crossroads is to look at some of the people who have successfully taken the difficult route ahead of me. I then smile, take a deep breath and say to myself 'if they can do it so can I'! Everything in life is relative Keith."

Alan: "As David says your personal confidence and the application of it is so very important with regard to almost every thing you do. I remember setting up my first company. I had to go out on a 'limb' and take some major decisions that, looking back, needed a lot of courage which I did not think I had. I did take that all important step however and never looked back. It has a cumulative effect because once you experience the 'buzz' of success your confidence increases rapidly. You will however get setbacks but again as David says your benchmarks will remind you that you can succeed because you have done it before."

Jean was laughing "When I went to see my bank manager to seek a loan for my first hairdressing business I was definitely operating outside my comfort zone. I didn't really have a business plan at all. I just told him that I was a successful type of person and he gave me the money. I never looked back as my confidence in my own abilities and skills improved dramatically! That was the confidence building stepping stone I needed to launch my businesses."

Lisa: "does that answer your question, Keith?"

Keith: "Yes, thanks everyone. Also my thanks to Jean and David for writing such a positive book because you both put your points across with direction and humour. There is so much 'doom and gloom' circulated by the press and the media these days, it makes such a refreshing change to read something so positive! I sincerely hope there will be a follow up book."

Jean: "Thank you Keith for your kind remarks. It is so good to get that sort of feedback and yes there will most certainly be a follow up. All the very best of luck to you!"

David:"Keith, before you go I must tell you what happened after the parachute jump. The insignia above the entrance to the parachute school is written in Latin and literally translated states 'Knowledge Dispels Fear'. Someone and to this day I suspect it was one of the students on my jump course, had written in white paint 'Ignorance is Bliss!'

"And before anybody asks I will categorically deny that it was me who did it!"

David was grinning,

Everyone in the studio burst out laughing but despite the

mirth, Graham had to interrupt to introduce the next caller.

9.48 am: Graham Bell. "Sharon from Carlisle rang to say it's a great book she really enjoyed it. Andy from Exeter texted and thought it was interesting but is worried that some of the theory might not be as simple as it is portrayed. Gary asks if there is a series and Mandy from Birmingham says that she thinks all older children should read it. We have had four e-mails again asking if there is a second book and one which said that although it can be quite a boring subject the authors make it interesting and positive. A company director from Glasgow was so impressed with the overall attitude of the publication he thinks that every company should buy the book and insist that their staff read it. Another company boss rang to say that he totally agrees with David and Alan that the first point of contact of any company is 'make or break'. Finally, a headmistress from London said that this publication should be readily available in all schools and educational establishments to help career and vocational planning. The message, especially to young people, that individual 'people and life skills' are so important to your advancement in life, is absolutely vital. She stated that many of her pupils who had read the book thought it was very interesting and extremely helpful."

"So, some interesting contacts. It would seem Lisa, that quite a few people agree with the ideology of this publication."

9.50 am: Lisa Houston. "Yes, thank you Graham. Jean I have an e-mail from Diane in Bedford. She says she sees from your web site that you are a qualified Life Coach. As a business lady she wants to know what advantages she would gain by contracting you as her own life coach?"

Jean: "Well Diane life coaching is a profession that has grown dramatically over the last ten years or so. Its heritage can be traced back to executive coaching in large corporate organisations. What has emerged is a profession that works with individual clients to help them achieve results and sustain life changing behaviour in their professional and private lives. The emphasis is always on producing action towards more fulfilment, more balance and a more effective way of living."

9.53 am: Lisa Houston. "Graham I think we have time for one more question."

Graham Bell: "The lady second row, second seat from the left."

"My name is Lydia. My question is for David and Jean. Your book is exceptionally positive. Surely it is not possible to be that positive all the time? What is the secret?"

David: "Hello Lydia. You are right, the book is positive because we are both positive people. We are very enthusiastic and passionate about every thing we do. My attitude is that we must all live our lives to the full and our enthusiasm has to be evident at work and play The whole ideology of our publication is that if you fulfil your potential then you are a much happier person because you will achieve so much more in your life. You owe it to yourself to achieve that potential and never ever let anyone convince you otherwise!"

Jean: "Yes Lydia I agree with you; despite being a positive person I find it is impossible to feel positive all the time. What I try to do however if I am having a negative moment is to allow myself that indulgence for just a short time. I then give myself a good talking to, tell myself to stop feeling sorry for myself and see which is the best way to deal with the problem. Then I get off my backside and get on with it. This shift in attitude soon gets me back on track."

Alan: "Lydia when you are in business you have to be positive because if you don't believe in yourself nobody else will. If you join a business networking group you can virtually feel the positive vibes from the more successful representatives. My company in house training concentrates on personal confidence and positivity as well as professional knowledge, expertise and of course customer service; it is mandatory."

9.57 am: Lisa Houston. "That's all we have time for this morning. Our thanks to Jean Sinnett and David Jones, Alan Johnson, our studio audience and of course all our viewers. Jesica Smyth will be here next with the news followed by Steve Long with all the sport. So it's goodbye from Graham Bell and me Lisa Houston; tune in next week at the same time when Jean and David will be back in the studio to answer more of your questions. Our special guest will be John Bradford who is the senior media consultant for one of the largest PR companies in the UK.

TO BE CONTINUED

Acknowledgements

Linda's cat Felix from Bristol. We can assure our readers that he is fit, well fed and as mischievous as ever. Oh, and so I understand is Linda now that she has all this spare time!

Jemima Duck and her 6 ducklings. They live on the banks of the river Severn near to the theatre at the Welsh Bridge in Shrewsbury. They now have their own 'duck billing'. On the side of the theatre is written in large type 'The Shrewsbury Severn' (Theatre). Who said humour is dead!

BOOKS

O is a symbol of the world, of oneness and unity. In different cultures it also means the "eye," symbolizing knowledge and insight. We aim to publish books that are accessible, constructive and that challenge accepted opinion, both that of academia and the "moral majority."

Our books are available in all good English language bookstores worldwide. If you don't see the book on the shelves ask the bookstore to order it for you, quoting the ISBN number and title. Alternatively you can order online (all major online retail sites carry our titles) or contact the distributor in the relevant country, listed on the copyright page.

See our website www.o-books.net for a full list of over 500 titles, growing by 100 a year.

And tune in to myspiritradio.com for our book review radio show, hosted by June-Elleni Laine, where you can listen to the authors discussing their books.

mySpiritRadio